SOME RECENT RESEARCHES IN THE THEORY OF STATISTICS AND ACTUARIAL SCIENCE

SOME RECENT RESEARCHES IN THE THEORY OF STATISTICS AND ACTUARIAL SCIENCE

BY

J. F. STEFFENSEN

Professor of Actuarial Science in the University of Copenhagen and Corresponding Member of the Institute of Actuaries London

CAMBRIDGE

Published for the Institute of Actuaries

AT THE UNIVERSITY PRESS

1930

CAMBRIDGE
UNIVERSITY PRESS

University Printing House, Cambridge CB2 8BS, United Kingdom

Cambridge University Press is part of the University of Cambridge.

It furthers the University's mission by disseminating knowledge in the pursuit of education, learning and research at the highest international levels of excellence.

www.cambridge.org
Information on this title: www.cambridge.org/9781316601914

First published 1930
First paperback edition 2015

A catalogue record for this publication is available from the British Library

ISBN 978-1-316-60191-4 Paperback

CONTENTS

Preface . . . . *page* vii

Lecture I 1

Introductory observations on the place of mathematics in Statistical and Actuarial Theory

Errors due to neglect of the principle that theoretical assumptions should not contain contradictions, illustrated by a discussion of (1) the Biometric functions; the doctrine of the "oldest age"; (2) the problem of two different mortality tables which produce identical policy values; (3) presumptive values of frequency-constants

Lecture II 21

A mathematical investigation of the limits of error in the calculation of $\bar{a}_x$ when the force of mortality follows Makeham's Law

A proposition in inequalities; with applications to Tchebychef's inequality, to the value of $\bar{e}_x$, to the values of temporary life annuities, to the policy values of endowment assurances, and to the paid-up policy that can be granted for a pure endowment

Lecture III 35

The theoretical foundation of various types of frequency-functions. The English School; Karl Pearson's types. The Continental School; the *A*-series; Charlier's *B*-series. Some notes on factorial moments

Notation 49

Index 51

PREFACE

The three Lectures delivered by the writer in London University on March 12th, 13th and 14th, 1930, are here presented together in a somewhat extended form. In publishing these Lectures I have supplied all such details as had to be left out, owing to the limited time at my disposal. In order that the present publication may be read by itself, I have also found it advisable to include certain details which are already accessible in other papers of mine.

My best thanks are due to the Institute of Actuaries for facilitating this publication.

J. F. STEFFENSEN

COPENHAGEN

March 1930

First Lecture

1. When, some time ago, I had the honour of receiving an invitation to deliver in the University of London a course of lectures on a subject connected with Statistics, I felt a certain hesitation about accepting, because I am not so much a statistician as an actuary. As, however, the subject on which I was invited to lecture was not termed "statistics" without further qualification, but was only to be a subject "connected with" statistics, I thought I might accept after all, as most of what I have written is concerned with that borderland between statistics and mathematics which constitutes actuarial science. I therefore propose to give an account of some of the efforts I have made to introduce more rigour into certain questions of theoretical statistics and actuarial science, drawing my examples from widely different sources. It will be convenient to begin with a few remarks about the place of mathematics in statistical and actuarial science.

The first point of view that occurs to the mind is that mathematics, even when applied to observed data, is a science that investigates *the relations which exist between numbers*. Observations may contradict each other, owing to unavoidable errors of observation, but mathematical relations are not allowed to contain contradictions. Statistical and actuarial theory must therefore always be presented in such a form that the theoretical relations or assumptions contain no contradiction. In this first lecture I intend to show by examples how we may be led astray by neglect of this principle.

In the second place, mathematics is the proper instrument for justifying *methods of numerical approximation*. Such methods frequently originate in practical work where some approximate method has been found to produce satisfactory results. But too often the computer leaves the matter at that and takes it for granted that the results will be equally satisfactory in other cases. He treats the problem as a statistical one, while its nature is purely mathematical. More or less consciously he obliterates the profound difference between interpolation and graduation, and combines both into a single calculus of observations. It is hardly an exaggeration to say that it is a universal habit amongst actuaries and statisticians to regard a formula of approximation as definitely established when good results have been obtained in a few trial cases. In the second lecture we will consider some questions of this nature, and also occupy ourselves with the allied subject of numerical inequalities.

Thirdly, mathematics is employed for *describing facts of observation*. The formulas used in statistics for this purpose are often of an entirely empirical nature. But there are also cases where theoretical reasons can be given for believing that one formula will fit the facts better than another; and much work can then be saved by choosing from the outset the most suitable formula. It is therefore of considerable practical importance to investigate the theoretical foundation of formulas derived by speculation. Striking examples of such formulas are the types of frequency-functions which will be discussed in the third and last lecture.

2. I shall begin by a critical examination of the notion of *Biometric Functions*. I have dealt with this subject on an earlier occasion*, but before a mathematical rather than a statistical audience, so that I feel justified in recapitulating my views here and illustrating them with an application.

Before going into the objections which can be raised against the manner in which these questions are usually dealt with, I will rather introduce the biometric functions in a way which does not seem open to serious objection.

Let us consider a group of individuals of the same age x and selected according to the same principle with respect to the other essential factors affecting mortality, so that the group may be looked upon as an aggregate of *repeated observations*. Under these circumstances we may assume the existence of such a function μ_x, continuous for all ages $x > 0$, that $\mu_x dx$ represents the probability for a life aged x of dying between the ages x and $x + dx$. The existence of this function—the *force of mortality*—is a postulate, but one which is supported by the evidence of experience; for the causes of death are either constant for all ages (many forms of accidents), or else dependent on the way in which the organism develops and finally wears out, and this process is of a continuous nature.

Very little can be said *a priori* about the function μ_x. Perhaps the only statement that can be made without consulting mortality observations is that there must exist a positive constant ϵ, *independent of* x, such that

$$\mu_x \geqslant \epsilon > 0 \qquad (x \geqslant 0). \qquad ......(1)$$

For a lower limit to μ_x, greater than zero, can at least be derived from the probability of dying by accident. The simple fact expressed by (1) is, however, as we shall presently see, of considerable importance.

* *Proceedings of the Sixth Scandinavian Congress of Mathematicians*, pp. 329–343.

By means of the force of mortality the other biometric functions may be obtained as follows. Let there be l_x persons alive at age x. The mathematical expectation of death amongst these persons in the interval from x to $x + dx$ is $l_x \mu_x dx$. The expected number of living at the end of the interval dx is, therefore,

$$l_{x+dx} = l_x - l_x \mu_x dx,$$

whence $$\mu_x = -\frac{1}{l_x}\frac{dl_x}{dx} = -D \operatorname{Log} l_x, \qquad \text{......(2)}$$

where D denotes the operation of differentiation, and Log the natural logarithm.

Integrating (2), we obtain for the probability that a person aged x is alive after the time t

$${}_tp_x = \frac{l_{x+t}}{l_x} = e^{-\int_x^{x+t} \mu_x dx}, \qquad \text{......(3)}$$

whence in particular, for $t = 1$,

$$p_x = e^{-\int_x^{x+1} \mu_x dx} \qquad \text{......(4)}$$

while the probability of dying within a year is $q_x = 1 - p_x$.

If, in (3), we put $x = \alpha$ and thereafter $t = x - \alpha$, we find

$$l_x = l_\alpha e^{-\int_\alpha^x \mu_x dx}. \qquad \text{......(5)}$$

3. Before proceeding, let us see what general conclusions can be drawn from these results, concerning the nature of the biometric functions.

It follows from (3) and (1) that, as t increases, the probability of surviving, ${}_tp_x$, decreases in a monotonic sense to zero without attaining this value for any finite value of t.

From (1) and (5)—where l_α may be considered as an arbitrary constant—it may be concluded that, as x increases, the function l_x decreases in a monotonic sense to zero without attaining this value for any finite value of x. We may even say something about the rapidity of this decrease; for we have

$$l_x < l_\alpha e^{-(x-\alpha)\epsilon} \qquad (x > \alpha), \qquad \text{......(6)}$$

which shows that the decrease is, at least, so rapid that all the *moments*

$$\int_\alpha^\infty x^r l_x dx$$

and the *repeated integrals*

$$\int_\alpha^\infty \int_x^\infty \cdots \int_x^\infty l_x dx^r$$

are necessarily convergent.

The interesting question, whether $\mu_x \to \infty$ as $x \to \infty$, cannot be decided either by observation or by speculation. We obtain from (4), by the theorem of mean value,

$$q_x = 1 - e^{-\mu_\xi} \quad (x < \xi < x + 1). \qquad \ldots\ldots(7)$$

From this relation, it follows that $\mu_x \to \infty$ as $q_x \to 1$ and *vice versa*. But whether $q_x \to 1$ as $x \to \infty$ is impossible to decide. All that can be said is that this assumption, if desired, can be made without introducing any contradiction.

There is every reason to believe that above a certain age the function μ_x *does not decrease*. As, by (4),

$$-\operatorname{Log} p_x = \int_x^{x+1} \mu_x dx,$$

we have under these circumstances

$$\mu_x \leqslant -\operatorname{Log} p_x \leqslant \mu_{x+1}. \qquad \ldots\ldots(8)$$

But, as
$$\begin{aligned} -\operatorname{Log} p_x &= -\operatorname{Log}(1 - q_x) \\ &= q_x + \tfrac{1}{2}q_x^2 + \tfrac{1}{3}q_x^3 + \ldots, \end{aligned}$$

it follows from (8) that

$$q_x < \mu_{x+1}, \qquad \ldots\ldots(9)$$

provided only that μ_x does not decrease in the interval from x to $x + 1$. As q_x and μ_x do not differ greatly for the ages which are of practical importance, this simple inequality will often be found useful.

4. Another important biometric function is the *expectation of life* $\bar{e}_x$, defined by

$$\bar{e}_x = \int_0^\infty {}_tp_x dt = \frac{1}{l_x}\int_x^\infty l_x dx. \qquad \ldots\ldots(10)$$

We may also, by (3), express the expectation of life in terms of μ_x, thus

$$\bar{e}_x = \int_0^\infty e^{-\int_x^{x+t} \mu_x dx} dt. \qquad \ldots\ldots(11)$$

Inserting the lower limit to μ_x by (1), we obtain, on performing the integration,

$$\bar{e}_x \leqslant \frac{1}{\epsilon}. \qquad \ldots\ldots(12)$$

That is, there exists a boundary, independent of x, which $\bar{e}_x$ cannot exceed. This result is trivial, but a more important inequality may be proved, if it is assumed that μ_x *never decreases for* $x \geqslant x_0$. In that case, it follows from (11) that

$$\bar{e}_x \leqslant \int_0^\infty e^{-t\mu_x}\,dt,$$

or

$$\bar{e}_x \leqslant \frac{1}{\mu_x} \quad (x \geqslant x_0), \qquad \text{......(13)}$$

whence, by (9),

$$\bar{e}_x < \frac{1}{q_{x-1}} \quad (x \geqslant x_0 + 1). \qquad \text{......(14)}$$

Instead of $\bar{e}_x$ it is often sufficient to consider the *curtate expectation of life* e_x defined by

$$e_x = \sum_{t=1}^{\infty} {}_tp_x = \frac{1}{l_x} \sum_{t=1}^{\infty} l_{x+t}, \qquad \text{......(15)}$$

which, as l_x is constantly decreasing, is always smaller than $\bar{e}_x$. We evidently have

$$e_x = p_x + p_x p_{x+1} + p_x p_{x+1} p_{x+2} + \dots,$$

so that, if p_x *does not increase with* x,

$$e_x \leqslant p_x + p_x^2 + p_x^3 + \dots,$$

or

$$e_x \leqslant \frac{p_x}{q_x}. \qquad \text{......(16)}$$

From (15) we immediately find

$$e_x = p_x (1 + e_{x+1}). \qquad \text{......(17)}$$

This relation shows that if $q_x \to 1$ for $x \to \infty$, then $e_x \to 0$ for $x \to \infty$, and conversely: if $e_x \to 0$, then $q_x \to 1$.

It follows that if $\bar{e}_x \to 0$, then $\mu_x \to \infty$. The converse proposition may be proved thus: If $\mu_x \to \infty$ as $x \to \infty$, we may choose x so large that $\mu_x > K$ for all values of x above a certain limit, and consequently by (11), $\bar{e}_x < \frac{1}{K}$ for all values of x above that limit. But K being arbitrary, we have $\bar{e}_x \to 0$ if $\mu_x \to \infty$.

5. What the text-books say about the function l_x is as a rule not expressed with sufficient reserve, and is even in many cases positively misleading. Without going into details about the various forms of vagueness or inaccuracy I have observed, I think it safe to assert that an ordinary student reading a text-book for the first time may be led to form the following opinions on the nature of the table of l_x.

Assume that l_0 persons are born, and that we follow these persons from their birth till their death, the number of those who are alive after x years being denoted by l_x. They will certainly all die within a finite time. There is therefore an "oldest age" ω such that $l_x > 0$ for $x < \omega$, and $l_x = 0$ for $x \geqslant \omega$. No question of convergence arises, for we have simply

$$\int_x^\infty l_x dx = \int_x^\omega l_x dx,$$

the limits of integration being in reality finite. If an analytical expression is assumed for l_x, it may safely be assumed that $\int_\omega^\infty$ is so small that it can be neglected.

Our student is confirmed in this view when he discovers that the table of l_x is stated in integral numbers, commencing with, say, 100,000 persons at the lowest age and terminating with 0 at an age about 100 years.

But this point of view contains a fallacy. It is true that any given *finite* number of persons must all die within a finite time or, to put it more precisely, the probability that one or more of them will survive indefinitely is zero. This follows from the above established fact that ${}_tp_x \to 0$ when $t \to \infty$. But the greater that number of persons is, the greater will also be the number of them who may still be alive at age 100 or any other assigned age, and it is therefore quite impossible to maintain the existence of any definite "oldest age" ω within which everybody must certainly die. Let us, to put it mathematically, assume for a moment that ω is the upper limit of the age which human life can attain. Then we have admitted that it is possible that a person may be alive at the age $\omega - \eta$, where η is a quantity which we may choose *as small as we please*, for instance equal to one second. But at the exact age ω, or one second later, that person must, according to hypothesis, necessarily be dead. Does anybody really believe that there is an age ω with this miraculous peculiarity?

It might, however, be argued that in introducing the function l_x in the way we have advocated above, we only replace one monstrosity by another, for we admit the possibility of a person being alive at any age, however advanced. Nobody will ever believe that a person can live to become 1000 years old, and from a practical point of view this may safely be maintained. It is *practically* immaterial whether we say that a person *cannot* attain the age of 1000 years, or that the *probability* of attaining that age* is $< 10^{-10^{35}}$, an inconceivably small number. But if

* According to the $O^{M(5)}$ table as graduated by Makeham's formula we have

$$\log l_x = 5{\cdot}0575047 - {\cdot}0025575x - 10^{{\cdot}039x + \bar{4}{\cdot}7007037},$$

whence, for instance,

$$\log \frac{l_{1000}}{l_{10}} < -10^{35}.$$

theoretical clearness can be gained by speaking of extremely small probabilities instead of impossibilities, it should certainly be done. Infinity is not a number, but only denotes the absence of a boundary, and the non-occurrence in practice of observations of a certain order of magnitude should not without necessity be attributed to a mysterious boundary hidden somewhere, as it is always sufficiently accounted for by their exceedingly small probabilities, exactly as in the Theory of Errors. Even in such an everyday subject as the Theory of Interest we do not hesitate to make use of infinite durations in cases where no boundary can be indicated, not because anybody believes that a perpetuity will really continue to be paid *ad infinitum*, but because it is a convenient and harmless construction, as the very distant payments do not appreciably influence the value of the perpetuity.

6. An entirely different point of view from the one we have discussed is that in actually constructing a table of l_x it is necessary to stop at a certain age which we may still call ω, although it has nothing to do with an "oldest age" in the abstract sense of the word. Our ω will now be determined, not by an imagined impossibility of living beyond that age, but by considering the error committed in calculating integrals and sums to the limit ω instead of to infinity.

It seems reasonable to determine ω in such a way that in calculating the expectation of life by the approximate formula

$$\bar{e}_x = \frac{1}{l_x}\int_x^{\omega} l_x\,dx \qquad \text{......(18)}$$

we obtain at least three reliable decimals in the result. In that case we must have

$$\frac{1}{l_x}\int_{\omega}^{\infty} l_x\,dx < \cdot 0005.$$

Assuming now that μ_x does not decrease for $x > \omega$, we have according to (13)

$$\int_{\omega}^{\infty} l_x\,dx < \frac{l_\omega}{\mu_\omega},$$

so that we shall have three correct decimals in $\bar{e}_x$ provided that

$$\frac{1}{l_x}\cdot\frac{l_\omega}{\mu_\omega} < \cdot 0005,$$

that is, if

$$l_x \geqslant 2000\,\frac{l_\omega}{\mu_\omega}.$$

It follows from this that we shall have at least three correct decimals in $\bar{e}_x$ calculated by (18), when $x \leqslant 100$, if ω is calculated by

$$l_{100} = 2000 \frac{l_\omega}{\mu_\omega}. \qquad \text{......(19)}$$

In the $O^{M(5)}$ table as graduated by Makeham's formula we have

$$\mu_x = \cdot 0058889 + 10^{\cdot 039x + \bar{4}\cdot 0161709};$$

by this and by the expression for log l_x given above we find $106 < \omega < 107$. The table of l_x must therefore be prolonged as far as 107 if we want the expectation of life with three correct decimals for all ages up to 100 years, neglecting the contribution from ages above 107. And—this is material—l_x should be given with a sufficient number of figures throughout, say five or six significant* figures, and not, as at present, finishing off with $l_{100} = 7$, $l_{101} = 3$, $l_{102} = 1$.

There are, of course, other ways of determining ω; we may, for instance, consider sums instead of integrals; or we may fix ω arbitrarily, in which case it would be necessary to investigate how many decimals in the expectation of life may be relied upon at the various ages. But in all cases the principle remains the same, and we need hardly go into further details.

It is sometimes objected that there is no meaning in stating l_x and similar functions with five significant figures at the highest ages, because the observations available there, even after graduation, are insufficient for producing this degree of accuracy, and also because the table is to be applied to the future which never agrees wholly with the past.

This question is closely connected with the question of the purpose of graduation. It may be said in a general way that the object of graduation is to replace the rough observations by a more "smooth" series of data; but the smoothness thus obtained is partly lost again, if the last few values of l_x are only stated with one or two significant figures. If now we proceed one step further and ask *why* we want the table to be smooth, the answer is: Not only, because a smooth table is likely to be closer to the truth than an irregular one, but chiefly because we want to be justified in applying methods of interpolation, numerical differentiation and integration, etc., in short *mathematical methods*, to the table. But this requires that the function represented by the table possesses a differential coefficient of a certain order, and the simplest way to ensure this is to graduate

* The "significant" figures commence with the first figure that is different from zero.

the table by an analytical function. Under these circumstances there is evidently a need for retaining a not too small number of figures throughout the table, and this number of figures has nothing to do with the accuracy of the observations. It depends on the use that is to be made of the table, and remains the same whether the table is a purely hypothetical one, or has been derived from a very large number of observations.

7. As an application of the principles discussed above, we will consider the classical problem: whether it is possible to have two different mortality tables producing, for all ages at entry and durations, the same policy values for a life assurance with annual premiums.

Denoting, as usual, the life annuity-due by a_x, and the policy value after t years by ${}_tV_x$, we have*

$$ {}_tV_x = 1 - \frac{a_{x+t}}{a_x}. \qquad \text{......(20)} $$

Let μ_x^{I} be the force of mortality according to another table of mortality; the corresponding life-annuities, etc., will be denoted by a_x^{I}, etc.

If, now, we are to have ${}_tV_x = {}_tV_x^{\mathrm{I}}$, we must, according to (20), have

$$ \frac{a_{x+t}}{a_{x+t}^{\mathrm{I}}} = \frac{a_x}{a_x^{\mathrm{I}}} \qquad \text{......(21)} $$

for all values of x and t. Denoting by k a constant, the condition (21) may therefore be written

$$ \frac{a_x}{a_x^{\mathrm{I}}} = 1 - k. \qquad \text{......(22)} $$

It is obvious that $k < 1$, as the expression on the left is always positive. But k must as a rule also satisfy another condition. Let us assume that the original mortality table has been graduated by such a formula (for instance Makeham's formula) that $\mu_x \to \infty$ as $x \to \infty$. This is, according to paragraph 3, equivalent to saying that $q_x \to 1$ as $x \to \infty$. We therefore have $a_x \to 1$ as $x \to \infty$, as follows from the obvious relation

$$ a_x = 1 + v p_x a_{x+1}, \qquad \text{......(23)} $$

where v is the present value of a unit, due one year hence. But if $a_x \to 1$, it follows from (22) that a_x^{I} tends to a limiting value that *exceeds* 1 (as $k < 1$). For $k = 0$ would mean that the two

* *Institute of Actuaries' Text-Book*, Part II, Second Ed. (1902), p. 323.

mortality tables, against hypothesis, were identical, and $k < 0$, that a_x^I could become smaller than unity. We therefore have $0 < k < 1$.

Let us now put

$$\lim_{x \to \infty} a_x^I = 1 + \eta \qquad (\eta > 0). \qquad \text{......(24)}$$

In the equation

$$a_x^I = 1 + vp_x^I a_{x+1}^I \qquad \text{......(25)}$$

we let $x \to \infty$ and introduce (24), putting $v = \frac{1}{1+i}$, where i is the rate of interest. We then have

$$1 + \eta = 1 + \frac{1+\eta}{1+i}(1 - q_\infty^I),$$

whence

$$q_\infty^I = \frac{1 - \eta i}{1 + \eta}. \qquad \text{......(26)}$$

A mortality table producing such annuity values a_x^I that (22) is satisfied must therefore be a peculiar one, as $q_\infty^I < 1$. It is easy to construct the table, for we obtain from (25)

$$p_x^I = \frac{a_x^I - 1}{va_{x+1}^I},$$

whence, as

$$a_x^I = \frac{a_x}{1-k} \quad \text{and} \quad a_{x+1}^I = \frac{a_{x+1}}{1-k},$$

$$p_x^I = \frac{a_x - 1 + k}{va_{x+1}}, \qquad \text{......(27)}$$

or, eliminating a_{x+1} by (23)

$$p_x^I = p_x\left(1 + \frac{k}{a_x - 1}\right). \qquad \text{......(28)}$$

This suffices for constructing the table of l_x^I. But we still have to satisfy ourselves that it is possible to give k such a value, comprised between 0 and 1, that all the values of p_x^I obtained from (28) are confined to the interval from 0 to 1, as otherwise they could not represent probabilities. Now, as k is positive, p_x^I is evidently always positive. The condition $p_x^I < 1$ can be written

$$k < \frac{q_x}{p_x}(a_x - 1),$$

or by (23)

$$k < vq_x a_{x+1}. \qquad \text{......(29)}$$

This inequality must be satisfied for all values of x, and besides we must have $0 < k < 1$. It is easy to see that values of k exist satisfying these conditions. We may, for instance, choose k so that $0 < k < vq$ where q is the lowest value which q_x assumes.

The restrictions on k derived above are by no means observed in the literature of the subject. Thus the condition $k > 0$, resulting from the behaviour of μ_x and μ_x^I at infinity, is disregarded in *Text-Book*, Ed. 1902, l.c., pp. 336–338, where a transformation of the mortality table is made with a *negative* value of k, putting

$$p_x^I = p_x\left(1 - \frac{\cdot 05}{\mathrm{a}_x - 1}\right),$$

although the original table (H^M, Text-Book graduation) is graduated by Makeham's formula, so that $\mathrm{a}_x \to 1$ as $x \to \infty$. The result is that the probabilities p_x^I become negative above a certain age, determined by $\mathrm{a}_x < 1{\cdot}05$. These negative probabilities have escaped detection, possibly because the probabilities p_x^I have only been calculated up to age 95. But even continuation beyond that age might have thrown no more light on the matter, as the annuity values at the higher ages are very unreliable, because the table of l_x is stated in integers ($l_{100} = 4$, $l_{101} = 1$, $l_{102} = 0$), an objectionable practice which we have criticised above.

8. Another statistical problem which is usually treated in such a way that it leads to contradictions is the question of *Presumptive Values of Frequency-Constants.* Let us begin by explaining wherein this problem consists.

Let there be n repeated observations o_i ($i = 1, 2, \dots n$). Any symmetrical function of *all* the observations, such as the moments about a given point, the semi-invariants, etc., will be called a "frequency-constant." We denote the rth moment about the origin, after division by n, by σ_r*, that is

$$\sigma_r = \frac{1}{n}\sum_{i=1}^{n} o_i^r, \qquad \text{......(30)}$$

so that, in particular, $\sigma_0 = 1$, while σ_1 is the arithmetical *mean* of the observations.

Further, we denote by m_r the moments about the mean, after dividing by n, that is

$$m_r = \frac{1}{n}\sum_{i=1}^{n} (o_i - \sigma_1)^r \qquad (r > 1). \qquad \text{......(31)}$$

For $r = 1$ we define $m_1 = \sigma_1$.

* A folding sheet at the end of this publication gives the notation used by me: English readers will notice that it differs from that customary in their country.

The functions σ_r as well as m_r are examples of frequency-constants. We may for the moment confine our attention to these two classes. It is well known that they are absolutely equivalent: from $\sigma_1, \sigma_2, \dots \sigma_\kappa$ we may calculate $m_1, m_2, \dots m_\kappa$, and *vice versa*. Further, that the first n values of σ_r (or m_r) are equivalent to the n observations which may be calculated from them*.

If the number of trials n is allowed to increase indefinitely, the values of σ_r, being arithmetical means of the o_i^r, are supposed to tend to certain limits which we shall call the *true values* (in a purely mathematical sense) and shall denote by $\bar{\sigma}_r$. At the same time the values of m_r will, on account of their relations with those of σ_r, tend to their true values $\bar{m}_r$.

The question now arises: What approximations shall we use instead of the true values, if we do not know these *a priori* but only have the observations to go by? Such approximations, if any can be found, are what is meant by the expression "presumptive values" of frequency-constants.

The search for presumptive values goes back to no less an authority than Gauss, who recommended, *faute de mieux*, to put†

$$\bar{m}_2 = \frac{n}{n-1} m_2, \qquad \text{......(32)}$$

while no better value than m_1 could be found for $\bar{m}_1$.

As the argument by which (32) is obtained is constantly recurring in deriving various kinds of presumptive values, we may as well reproduce it here.

We have

$$m_2 = \sigma_2 - \sigma_1^2 = \frac{1}{n}\Sigma o_i^2 - \frac{1}{n^2}(\Sigma o_i)^2,$$

which may be written

$$m_2 = \frac{1}{n}\left(1 - \frac{1}{n}\right)\Sigma o_i^2 - \frac{2}{n^2}\Sigma o_i o_j \qquad (i \neq j). \qquad \text{......(33)}$$

As m_2 is a function of observations, it may itself be looked upon as an observation. The true value of an m_2 calculated by n observations o_i is, of course, not the same thing as $\bar{m}_2$, as it depends on n. It may be denoted by $\bar{m}_1(m_2)$, or, perhaps more simply, by $E(m_2)$, being in fact the *mathematical expectation* of an m_2 calculated by n observations.

In calculating $E(m_2)$ we make use of the well-known theorems that the expectation of a sum is equal to the sum of the expecta-

* Thiele, *Theory of Observations*, pp. 23–24.

† As $\bar{m}_2$ denotes the *true* value, a new symbol should strictly be introduced for denoting the *presumptive* value. We trust however that no confusion will arise from using the same symbol.

tions, and that, if the observations are mutually independent, the expectation of a product is equal to the product of the expectations.

We now obtain from (33), remembering that o_i and o_j are independent of each other, as we have assumed $i \neq j$,

$$E(m_2) = \frac{1}{n}\left(1 - \frac{1}{n}\right) \Sigma E(o_i^2) - \frac{2}{n^2} \Sigma E(o_i) E(o_j);$$

but for any given value of i we have $E(o_i) = \overline{\sigma}_1$, $E(o_i^2) = \overline{\sigma}_2$; and as the number of terms in the first sum is n, in the second $\binom{n}{2}$, we find

$$E(m_2) = \frac{1}{n}\left(1 - \frac{1}{n}\right) n\overline{\sigma}_2 - \frac{2}{n^2}\binom{n}{2}\overline{\sigma}_1^2$$

$$= \frac{n-1}{n}(\overline{\sigma}_2 - \overline{\sigma}_1^2),$$

or

$$E(m_2) = \frac{n-1}{n}\overline{m}_2. \qquad \text{......(34)}$$

This is an exact formula, resting on the assumption that we have an infinity of *sets* of observations o_i with n observations in each set. If we have only one set of observations o_i, we must instead of $E(m_2)$ take m_2, exactly as, if we have only one observation o_1, we are compelled to use this as an approximation to $\overline{\sigma}_1$. We thus have the approximate relation

$$m_2 = \frac{n-1}{n}\overline{m}_2,$$

whence follows at once the Gaussian presumptive value (32).

In the same way we obtain from (30)

$$E(\sigma_r) = \frac{1}{n}\sum_{i=1}^{n} E(o_i^r);$$

but $E(o_i^r) = \overline{\sigma}_r$ for any given value of i, so that $E(\sigma_r) = \frac{1}{n} \cdot n\overline{\sigma}_r$,

or

$$E(\sigma_r) = \overline{\sigma}_r. \qquad \text{......(35)}$$

Hence, we have the presumptive values

$$\overline{\sigma}_r = \sigma_r. \qquad \text{......(36)}$$

It follows, in particular, that $\overline{m}_1 = m_1$. But (32) shows that we do *not* in general have $\overline{m}_r = m_r$. We find, by the same method, leaving out the details of the calculation,

$$E(m_3) = \frac{(n-1)(n-2)}{n^2}\overline{m}_3, \qquad \text{......(37)}$$

$$E(m_4) = \frac{n-1}{n^3}[(n^2 - 3n + 3)\overline{m}_4 + 3(2n-3)\overline{m}_2^2]. \qquad \text{......(38)}$$

If now we replace $E(m_3)$ by m_3, and $E(m_4)$ by m_4, using for $\overline{m}_2$ the already found presumptive value (32), we have as far as $\overline{m}_4$ the presumptive values

$$\left.\begin{aligned} \overline{m}_1 &= m_1 \\ \overline{m}_2 &= \frac{n}{n-1} m_2 \\ \overline{m}_3 &= \frac{n^2}{(n-1)(n-2)} m_3 \\ \overline{m}_4 &= \frac{n^3}{(n-1)(n^2-3n+3)} \left[m_4 - \frac{3(2n-3)}{n(n-1)} m_2^2 \right] \end{aligned}\right\} \quad \ldots\ldots(39)$$

which we shall call *Thiele's presumptive values*, because the corresponding values for semi-invariants (agreeing as far as $\overline{m}_3$ with the above) were first given by Thiele, who has even calculated them as far as the 8th semi-invariant*.

9. We proceed to examine what objections may be raised to this way of deriving presumptive values of frequency-constants.

Confining ourselves to the first two moments, which is sufficient for our purpose, we first call attention to the fact that the knowledge of σ_1 and σ_2 is absolutely equivalent to the knowledge of m_1 and m_2; for from σ_1 and σ_2 we may calculate m_1 and m_2, and *vice versa*, by the relations

$$\left.\begin{aligned} m_1 &= \sigma_1 \\ m_2 &= \sigma_2 - \sigma_1^2 \end{aligned}\right\} \qquad \left.\begin{aligned} \sigma_1 &= m_1 \\ \sigma_2 &= m_2 + m_1^2 \end{aligned}\right\} \quad \ldots\ldots(40)$$

which evidently also hold for the true values $\overline{\sigma}_1, \overline{\sigma}_2, \overline{m}_1, \overline{m}_2$. If, for some purposes, we prefer m_1 and m_2 to σ_1 and σ_2, it is not because m_1 and m_2 contain more information about the observations, but because the information is contained in a more convenient *form*; thus m_2 is an approximation to the square of the standard deviation; is usually written with fewer figures than σ_2; is easier to calculate; etc. But this being so, it becomes extremely improbable that m_1 and m_2 can tell us something about the true values of the first two moments which σ_1 and σ_2 cannot also tell us. It is therefore a very suspicious fact that if we try to derive $\overline{\sigma}_2$ from σ_2 by the *same method* which is used for deriving $\overline{m}_2$ from m_2, we arrive at the result that σ_2 must be used *unaltered*, while instead of m_2 we must take $\frac{n}{n-1} m_2$ or $m_2 + \frac{m_2}{n-1}$. This suspicion is strengthened by the consideration

* Thiele, *Theory of Observations* (London, 1903), p. 48. Most of these results were given in the first (Danish) edition of that work (1889).

that the correction to be added to m_2, or $\frac{m_2}{n-1}$, is of a *smaller order of magnitude than the mean error of* m_2. For we have

$$\bar{m}_2(m_2) = E(m_2^2) - [E(m_2)]^2$$
$$= E(\sigma_2^2 - 2\sigma_2\sigma_1^2 + \sigma_1^4) - \left(\frac{n-1}{n}\bar{m}_2\right)^2,$$

which may be reduced to the well-known expression

$$\bar{m}_2(m_2) = \frac{n-1}{n^3}[(n-1)\bar{m}_4 - (n-3)\bar{m}_2^2],$$

so that the mean error of m_2 for increasing n is generally of the order $\frac{1}{\sqrt{n}}$.

But we may go further and assert that there is an actual *contradiction* present. For, as the presumptive values of $\bar{m}_2$, $\bar{m}_1$, $\bar{\sigma}_2$, $\bar{\sigma}_1$ have been obtained by the same method, they must be considered equally good. If, however, in the relation $\bar{m}_2 = \bar{\sigma}_2 - \bar{\sigma}_1^2$, we insert these presumptive values, we find

$$\frac{n}{n-1}m_2 = \sigma_2 - \sigma_1^2 = m_2,$$

or $\frac{n}{n-1} = 1$, which is absurd.

10. The contradiction is brought home in a practical way, if we assume that the problem is to determine the constants in a frequency-function, say, for the sake of simplicity, Gauss' law of error, by the method of moments which is here identical with the method of least squares. Gauss' formula contains two constants to be determined by the observations, so that we have to use the first two moments for their determination. If we write the formula in the form

$$y = \frac{1}{\sqrt{2\pi\gamma}}e^{-\frac{(x-\alpha)^2}{2\gamma}}, \qquad \text{......(41)}$$

we find, by the method of moments,

$$\bar{\sigma}_1 = \int_{-\infty}^{\infty} xydx = \alpha, \qquad \bar{\sigma}_2 = \int_{-\infty}^{\infty} x^2ydx = \gamma + \alpha^2,$$

whence $\alpha = \bar{m}_1$, $\gamma = \bar{m}_2$. If instead of these, we use their presumptive values m_1 and $\frac{n}{n-1}m_2$, we have

$$y = \frac{1}{\sqrt{2\pi m_2 n/(n-1)}}e^{-\frac{(x-m_1)^2}{2m_2 n/(n-1)}}. \qquad \text{......(42)}$$

But if we write Gauss' formula in the form

$$y = \frac{1}{\sqrt{2\pi(\beta - \alpha^2)}} e^{-\frac{(x-\alpha)^2}{2(\beta-\alpha^2)}}, \qquad \text{......(43)}$$

we have, by the method of moments,

$$\bar{\sigma}_1 = \int_{-\infty}^{\infty} xydx = \alpha, \qquad \bar{\sigma}_2 = \int_{-\infty}^{\infty} x^2ydx = \beta,$$

so that $\alpha = \bar{\sigma}_1$, $\beta = \bar{\sigma}_2$. Using for $\bar{\sigma}_1$ and $\bar{\sigma}_2$ their presumptive values σ_1 and σ_2, we have

$$y = \frac{1}{\sqrt{2\pi(\sigma_2 - \sigma_1^2)}} e^{-\frac{(x-\sigma_1)^2}{2(\sigma_2-\sigma_1^2)}},$$

or

$$y = \frac{1}{\sqrt{2\pi m_2}} e^{-\frac{(x-m_1)^2}{2m_2}}. \qquad \text{......(44)}$$

But the two formulas (44) and (42) are in contradiction to each other, and it is not possible for me to see why (42) should be preferred to (44). We have in both cases used presumptive values, calculated by the same method, for the frequency-constants by which the constants of the formula are expressed.

11. It might perhaps be thought that the contradiction involved in (44) and (42) is not of very great importance, as $\frac{n}{n-1}$ is generally close to unity. To this we would first of all say that even if there were no contradiction at all, the trouble of investigating formulas for presumptive values should be spared, if they do not mean an actual improvement of the result. But in order to show the danger of the mode of argument employed, we will introduce an arbitrary constant into the problem* enabling us, so to speak, to magnify the contradiction to any extent we please.

Let c be a constant to be chosen as we like. Instead of using the frequency-constants m_1 and m_2 we may just as well use θ_1 and θ_2 defined by

$$\left.\begin{aligned}\theta_1 &= m_1\\ \theta_2 &= m_2 + cm_1^2\end{aligned}\right\} \qquad \left.\begin{aligned}m_1 &= \theta_1\\ m_2 &= \theta_2 - c\theta_1^2\end{aligned}\right\}. \qquad \text{......(45)}$$

These relations show that θ_1 and θ_2 contain exactly the same information about the observations as m_1 and m_2 (or σ_1 and σ_2). The relations (45) evidently also hold for the true values $\bar{\theta}_1$, $\bar{\theta}_2$, $\bar{m}_1$, $\bar{m}_2$.

* *Matematisk Tidsskrift* (1923), pp. 72–76.

Writing θ_2 in the form

$$\theta_2 = (1 - c)\, m_2 + c\sigma_2,$$

we have
$$E(\theta_2) = (1 - c)\frac{n-1}{n}\bar{m}_2 + c\bar{\sigma}_2;$$

or, introducing

$$\bar{m}_2 = \bar{\theta}_2 - c\bar{\theta}_1^2 \quad \text{and} \quad \bar{\sigma}_2 = \bar{\theta}_2 + (1 - c)\,\bar{\theta}_1^2,$$

$$E(\theta_2) = \left(1 - \frac{1-c}{n}\right)\bar{\theta}_2 + \frac{c(1-c)}{n}\bar{\theta}_1^2 \quad \text{......(46)}$$

besides the obvious relation

$$E(\theta_1) = \bar{\theta}_1. \quad \text{......(47)}$$

According to the general principle, we must, on the left of (47) and (46), replace $E(\theta_1)$ and $E(\theta_2)$ by θ_1 and θ_2 respectively. We thus obtain the presumptive values

$$\left.\begin{aligned} \bar{\theta}_1 &= \theta_1 \\ \bar{\theta}_2 &= \frac{n\theta_2 - c(1-c)\,\theta_1^2}{n - 1 + c} \end{aligned}\right\}. \quad \text{......(48)}$$

Nothing prevents us from writing Gauss' formula in the form

$$y = \frac{1}{\sqrt{2\pi(\beta - c\alpha^2)}}\, e^{-\frac{(x-\alpha)^2}{2(\beta - c\alpha^2)}}, \quad \text{......(49)}$$

where c is a *given* (arbitrarily chosen) constant, and determining the two unknown constants α and β by the method of moments. We find $\bar{\sigma}_1 = \alpha$, $\bar{\sigma}_2 = \beta + (1 - c)\,\alpha^2$, whence $\bar{m}_1 = \alpha$, $\bar{m}_2 = \beta - c\alpha^2$, so that, by (45), $\bar{\theta}_1 = \alpha$, $\bar{\theta}_2 = \beta$. Taking for $\bar{\theta}_1$ and $\bar{\theta}_2$ their presumptive values (48), we have

$$\left.\begin{aligned} \alpha &= m_1 \\ \beta &= \frac{n\theta_2 - c(1-c)\,\theta_1^2}{n - 1 + c} = \frac{nm_2}{n - 1 + c} + cm_1^2 \end{aligned}\right\}. \quad \text{...(50)}$$

Inserting these in (49), we finally have

$$y = \frac{1}{\sqrt{2\pi m_2 n/(n - 1 + c)}}\, e^{-\frac{(x - m_1)^2}{2m_2 n/(n-1+c)}}. \quad \text{...(51)}$$

But this result is obviously absurd. It is equivalent to taking as presumptive value for $\bar{m}_2$

$$\bar{m}_2 = \frac{n}{n - 1 + c} m_2, \quad \text{......(52)}$$

with an *arbitrary* value of c. Choosing for c a sufficiently large positive value, we get for $\overline{m}_2$ a value as small as we please; and choosing for c a sufficiently large negative value we get such an absurdity as a negative value of the square of a standard deviation, besides imaginary values for y.

12. Another definition of the presumptive value of a frequency-constant has been given by Tschuprow*. Let F be the true value of a function of observations, and let G be such a function of the observations that the mathematical expectation of G is equal to F; then G is the presumptive value of F.

Hence we have in symbols†

$$E(G) = F. \qquad \text{......(53)}$$

Tschuprow's presumptive values of the first four moments about the mean are‡

$$\left.\begin{aligned} \overline{m}_1 &= m_1 \\ \overline{m}_2 &= \frac{n}{n-1} m_2 \\ \overline{m}_3 &= \frac{n^2}{(n-1)(n-2)} m_3 \\ \overline{m}_4 &= \frac{n}{(n-1)(n-2)(n-3)} [(n^2 - 2n + 3) m_4 - 3(2n-3) m_2^2] \end{aligned}\right\}. \qquad \text{......(54)}$$

Of these, the first three agree with Thiele's presumptive values (39), while there is a difference in the fourth.

The difference between Thiele's and Tschuprow's methods may briefly be characterized thus:

According to Thiele, we must first calculate $E(m_r)$ as a function of $\overline{m}_1, \overline{m}_2, \dots \overline{m}_r$, that is

$$E(m_r) = \psi(\overline{m}_1, \overline{m}_2, \dots \overline{m}_r). \qquad \text{......(55)}$$

Dropping E, we have the presumptive equations

$$m_r = \psi(\overline{m}_1, \overline{m}_2, \dots \overline{m}_r), \qquad \text{......(56)}$$

from which the presumptive values $\overline{m}_1, \overline{m}_2, \dots$ can be found in succession for $r = 1, 2, \dots$.

* A. A. Tschuprow, *Grundbegriffe und Grundprobleme der Korrelationstheorie*, pp. 74–75; see also *Nordisk Statistisk Tidskrift* (1924), pp. 468–472.

† Two questions ought, strictly, to be cleared up, before proceeding with Tschuprow's method:

1. Is there always a solution to the equation (53)?
2. Can there be more than one solution?

For the following simple applications these questions are, however, of no importance.

‡ A number of similar results have been given quite recently by R. A. Fisher, "Moments and Product Moments of Sampling Distributions," *Proceedings of the London Mathematical Society*, Ser. 2, vol. XXX, Part 3, pp. 199–238.

According to Tschuprow, we must find such a function $\phi(m_1, m_2, \dots m_r)$ that

$$E(\phi) = \overline{m}_r. \qquad \dots\dots(57)$$

Dropping E, we have the presumptive values

$$\overline{m}_r = \phi(m_1, m_2, \dots m_r). \qquad \dots\dots(58)$$

There seems little to choose between the two methods, especially as the first three presumptive values are identical in the two cases. The objections raised above, founded on the presumptive value for $\overline{m}_2$, evidently apply equally to both methods.

13. Contradictions of a different nature from those discussed above have been detected by Mr N. P. Bertelsen*. Presumptive values of frequency-constants are obtained by introducing certain modifications into the frequency-constants obtained directly from the observations. These modifications must not, of course, be of such a nature that some or all of the observations to which the modified frequency-constants correspond are *imaginary*. The question whether the observations corresponding to *given* values of the frequency-constants are real, is the so-called question of the *compatibility of the frequency-constants*. A particularly simple case of incompatibility has already been mentioned above in connection with (52), as no real observations can produce a negative square of the standard deviation; even the value zero is only possible if all the observations have the same value.

Mr Bertelsen's analysis is too complicated to find a place here; we therefore confine ourselves to stating one of his results.

Let μ_r denote the rth semi-invariant, then the presumptive values of the first four semi-invariants are, in Tschuprow's sense,

$$\left.\begin{aligned}
\overline{\mu}_1 &= \mu_1 \\
\overline{\mu}_2 &= \frac{n}{n-1}\mu_2 \\
\overline{\mu}_3 &= \frac{n^2}{(n-1)(n-2)}\mu_3 \\
\overline{\mu}_4 &= \frac{n^2}{(n-1)(n-2)(n-3)}[(n+1)\mu_4 + 6\mu_2^2]
\end{aligned}\right\}. \qquad \dots\dots(59)$$

Mr Bertelsen proves that while the three first of these presumptive values are compatible, the fourth is not always compatible with the others.

* *Skandinavisk Aktuarietidskrift* (1927), pp. 129–156.

14. It appears thus that neither of the two systems of presumptive values of frequency-constants which have so far been proposed, respectively by Thiele and Tschuprow, is free from contradictions, and that a strong case can be made even against the time-honoured Gaussian formula $\overline{m}_2 = \frac{n}{n-1} m_2$. If, on the other hand, we use the uncorrected σ_r, m_r, μ_r, etc., as the best available approximations to $\overline{\sigma}_r$, $\overline{m}_r$, $\overline{\mu}_r$, etc., we are at least sure that no contradictions can ever be met with. In order to avoid contradictions, Tschuprow has suggested* that presumptive values ought never to be used for ordinary calculations; but one may well ask, why should we calculate presumptive values, if we may not use them in further calculations, e.g. for measuring the probability of errors, for determining the constants in frequency-functions, and so on.

* *Nordisk Statistisk Tidskrift* (1924), pp. 469–470.

Second Lecture

1. Let us assume that a table of $f(x)$ like that shown in the two first columns below is put before a computer with the request to calculate the value of $f(x)$ for $x = 4{\cdot}5$.

x	$f(x)$	δ	δ^2	δ^3	δ^4	δ^5	δ^6
1	99833						
		98836					
2	198669		− 1985				
		96851		− 968			
3	295520		− 2953		30		
		93898		− 938		9	
4	389418		− 3891		39		− 1
		90007		− 899		8	
5	479425		− 4790		47		+ 3
		85217		− 852		11	
6	564642		− 5642		58		
		79575		− 794			
7	644217		− 6436				
		73139					
8	717356						

(Note. In the table all values are multiplied by 10^6.)

Not knowing anything about the function except what he can see by the table itself, he will begin by forming the difference-table as shown, and having satisfied himself that the differences decrease very rapidly, it is more than likely that he will have no hesitation in interpolating as if the fifth or sixth difference were a constant, and stating the result as $f(4{\cdot}5) = {\cdot}434965$. All that he knows is, however, that this result is correct, if $f(x)$ is a polynomial of not more than the sixth degree, an hypothesis which can only be approximately true here, as the two values of the sixth difference obtainable are not equal to each other. The kind of certainty our computer possesses for the correctness of his result is therefore, strictly speaking, of a *statistical* nature: he has often interpolated under similar circumstances, and has probably never had reason to regret it.

If now we inform our computer that the function tabulated is

$$f(x) = \sin\frac{x}{10}, \qquad \ldots\ldots(1)$$

he will see no reason to alter his views; but if we tell him that it is

$$f(x) = \sin\frac{x}{10} + \sin \pi x, \qquad \ldots\ldots(2)$$

in which case $f(4{\cdot}5) = 1{\cdot}434965$, or that it is

$$f(x) = \sin\frac{x}{10} + x \sin \pi x, \qquad \ldots\ldots(3)$$

in which case $f(4{\cdot}5) = 4{\cdot}934965$, he will no doubt protest, and probably say that his method of interpolation is only intended for well-behaved functions. Yet the functions (2) and (3) are, in their way, just as inoffensive as (1), which shows that we cannot, without moving in a circle, define a "well-behaved" function as one to which our methods of interpolation apply.

The true source of the difficulty is that if we know nothing more about the function than what is given in the table, the function is *undefined* for any argument intermediate between those stated in the table. Therefore, if we insert a perfectly arbitrary value of $f(x)$ as corresponding to such an intermediate argument, no disagreement arises with the information contained in the table.

In order to obtain an approximation to the value of the function at such a place, it is not, however, necessary to know all about the function. As is shown in the text-books on interpolation*, it is sufficient to possess limits between which the derivate of a certain order is situated.

It follows from the preceding considerations that interpolation may be performed with two quite different objects in view which are, unfortunately, seldom kept sufficiently apart by practical computers.

In the first place, the object of an interpolation may be to find the value of a function for a certain value of the argument, the function being tabulated for certain other arguments, and *defined*, though not tabulated, for the intermediate arguments. This is a problem of *approximation*.

Secondly, the object of an interpolation may be to fill up, in a reasonable way, a gap in a given series of functional values, for a value of the argument where the function *is not defined*. This is a process which is much more akin to *graduation* than to interpolation and ought really to be called by a different name; we suggest the name *intercalation*. If, in such a case, the usual interpolation formulas are employed, they serve to define the function, not to approximate to it. We are here on hypothetical ground; we are more or less at liberty to accept or to reject the result of the intercalation on the ground of common-sense considerations, and there is no meaning in speaking of a greater or lesser "accuracy" of the result; "plausibility" would be the correct word. This is the case in a great many statistical applications of interpolation-formulas.

It is very unfortunate that the processes of interpolation and intercalation, because they happen to make use of the same mathematical instrument, have become mixed up in an almost

* See, for instance, J. F. Steffensen: *Interpolation* (Baltimore, 1927).

inextricable way in most text-books and papers dealing with interpolation. But it is only fair to admit that the temptation has often been considerable. As is shown in the theory of interpolation, the accuracy of an interpolation depends on the remainder term of the formula applied, and this remainder term can in a great many cases be presented in the form

$$R = Kf^{(n)}(\xi). \qquad \ldots\ldots(4)$$

But simple as this form is, it is often a difficult mathematical problem to derive sufficiently narrow *numerical* limits therefrom. And at a time when such numerical limits are only known in a comparatively small number of cases, the temptation is great to treat the problem throughout as a problem of intercalation. Thus it happens that even tables of simple and fundamental functions are often constructed without giving a thought to the remainder term, and yet the results are presented as if they were mathematically proved facts.

In my opinion, the most urgent problem that has to be faced by those who deal with numerical approximations, is to find suitable limits to (4) for the functions with which they are particularly concerned. As an example, I proceed to give a brief account of how this can be done for a function which is of extreme importance in actuarial science.

2. Let us assume that the force of mortality has been graduated by Makeham's formula

$$\mu_x = A + Be^{\gamma x}, \qquad \ldots\ldots(5)$$

so that the life table is represented by

$$l_x = ke^{-Ax - \frac{B}{\gamma}e^{\gamma x}}, \qquad \ldots\ldots(6)$$

where the constant k may be chosen arbitrarily. If we put

$$\frac{B}{\gamma}e^{\gamma x} = e^z, \qquad \ldots\ldots(7)$$

l_x assumes the form

$$l_x = Ke^{-\frac{A}{\gamma}z - e^z}, \qquad \ldots\ldots(8)$$

where K denotes another constant.

As $\dfrac{d}{dx} = \gamma\dfrac{d}{dz}$, it is seen that to find the nth derivate of l_x is essentially the same thing as finding the nth derivate of the function $e^{\theta z - e^z}$, where θ denotes a constant. Let us first consider this problem*.

* *Skandinavisk Aktuarietidskrift* (1928), pp. 75–97.

3. If the function

$$\phi(z) = e^{\theta z - e^z} \qquad \text{......(9)}$$

is differentiated n times, we obtain $\phi(z)$ multiplied by a polynomial of degree n in e^z and θ. Denoting this polynomial by $G_n(e^z, \theta)$, we have

$$\phi^{(n)}(z) = G_n(e^z, \theta)\,\phi(z). \qquad \text{......(10)}$$

Now, by Taylor's theorem

$$\phi(z+t) = \sum_{n=0}^{\infty} \phi^{(n)}(z) \frac{t^n}{n!},$$

whence, by (10) and (9),

$$\frac{\phi(z+t)}{\phi(z)} = e^{\theta t - e^z(e^t - 1)} = \sum_{n=0}^{\infty} G_n(e^z, \theta) \frac{t^n}{n!}.$$

Putting

$$\zeta = e^z, \qquad \text{......(11)}$$

we therefore have

$$e^{\theta t - (e^t - 1)\zeta} = \sum_{n=0}^{\infty} G_n(\zeta, \theta) \frac{t^n}{n!}. \qquad \text{......(12)}$$

The function on the left of this equation is, therefore, the *generating function* for the polynomials $G_n(\zeta, \theta)$. These are completely determined either by (10) or by (12).

The polynomials $G_n(\zeta, \theta)$ possess many interesting properties and deserve to be studied for their own sake. Here we content ourselves with deriving certain relations which are of importance for the following applications.

By differentiation of (10) we obtain, as $\phi'(z) = (\theta - e^z)\,\phi(z)$,

$$\phi^{(n+1)}(z) = \phi(z)\,[D_z G_n(e^z, \theta) + (\theta - e^z)\,G_n(e^z, \theta)],$$

and from this, by (10),

$$G_{n+1}(e^z, \theta) = D_z G_n(e^z, \theta) + (\theta - e^z)\,G_n(e^z, \theta);$$

or, as $D_z = \zeta D_\zeta$,

$$G_{n+1}(\zeta, \theta) = \zeta D_\zeta G_n(\zeta, \theta) + (\theta - \zeta)\,G_n(\zeta, \theta). \qquad \text{....(13)}$$

This is a recurrence formula which enables us to calculate the polynomials $G_n(\zeta, \theta)$ in succession, the initial value $G_0(\zeta, \theta) = 1$ resulting immediately from (10).

It is now easy to prove that

$$G_n(\zeta, \theta) = \sum_{s=0}^{n} (-1)^s \frac{\zeta^s}{s!} \Delta^s \theta^n, \qquad \text{......(14)}$$

where the difference-symbol Δ acts on θ. For this formula is valid for $n = 0$; and being valid for any particular value of n, it is proved by induction, by means of (13), that it is also valid for the following value.

An important relation is obtained by differentiating (12) with respect to ζ. We find

$$\sum_{n=0}^{\infty} D_\zeta G_n(\zeta, \theta) \frac{t^n}{n!} = -(e^t - 1)\, e^{\theta t - (e^t - 1)\zeta}$$
$$= e^{\theta t - (e^t - 1)\zeta} - e^{(\theta + 1)t - (e^t - 1)\zeta}$$
$$= \sum_{n=0}^{\infty} [G_n(\zeta, \theta) - G_n(\zeta, \theta + 1)] \frac{t^n}{n!},$$

so that $$D_\zeta G_n(\zeta, \theta) = G_n(\zeta, \theta) - G_n(\zeta, \theta + 1). \quad \text{......(15)}$$

If we compare this formula with (13), we find that

$$G_{n+1}(\zeta, \theta) = \theta G_n(\zeta, \theta) - \zeta G_n(\zeta, \theta + 1). \quad \text{......(16)}$$

By means of this formula we may prove that, in factorial notation,

$$| G_n(\zeta, \theta) | \leqslant (|\zeta| + |\theta| + n - 1)^{(n)}. \quad \text{......(17)}$$

For this formula is valid for $n = 0$; and being valid for some particular value of n, we find for the following one, by (16),

$$\begin{aligned} | G_{n+1}(\zeta, \theta)| &\leqslant |\theta| (|\zeta| + |\theta| + n - 1)^{(n)} \\ &\quad + |\zeta| (|\zeta| + |\theta + 1| + n - 1)^{(n)} \\ &\leqslant |\theta| (|\zeta| + |\theta| + n - 1)^{(n)} \\ &\quad + |\zeta| (|\zeta| + |\theta| + n)^{(n)} \\ &\leqslant (|\zeta| + |\theta| + n)^{(n)} (|\zeta| + |\theta|); \end{aligned}$$

or $$| G_{n+1}(\zeta, \theta)| \leqslant (|\zeta| + |\theta| + n)^{(n+1)},$$

so that (17) is also valid for the following value of n.

From (17) we may derive a more convenient, though less close, inequality. As the geometrical mean of positive quantities is not larger than the arithmetical mean, we have, for $a > 0$,

$$[a(a+1) \dots (a+n-1)]^{\frac{1}{n}} \leqslant \frac{1}{n}[a + (a+1) + \dots + (a+n-1)]$$

or $$[a(a+1) \dots (a+n-1)]^{\frac{1}{n}} \leqslant a + \frac{n-1}{2},$$

that is $$(a+n-1)^{(n)} \leqslant \left(a + \frac{n-1}{2}\right)^n \qquad (a > 0).$$

Applying this to (17), we find

$$| G_n(\zeta, \theta) | \leqslant \left(|\zeta| + |\theta| + \frac{n-1}{2}\right)^n. \quad \text{......(18)}$$

Although the limits to $G_n(\zeta, \theta)$ resulting from this inequality are very rough, it may occasionally, as we shall see, render good service.

4. Returning to the actuarial applications, we now obtain immediately from (8), by (10),

$$l_x^{(n)} = l_x \gamma^n G_n\left(e^z, -\frac{A}{\gamma}\right);$$

or, by (11), (7) and (5),

$$l_x^{(n)} = l_x \gamma^n G_n\left(\zeta, -\frac{A}{\gamma}\right), \qquad \text{......(19)}$$

$$\zeta = \frac{B}{\gamma} e^{\gamma x} = \frac{\mu_x - A}{\gamma}. \qquad \text{......(20)}$$

Further, let δ be the force of interest, and D_x the commutation function*

$$D_x = e^{-\delta x} l_x. \qquad \text{......(21)}$$

A glance at (6) shows that, in a table graduated by Makeham's formula, we pass from l_x to D_x by replacing A by $A + \delta$. As ζ thus remains unchanged, we have, by (19),

$$D_x^{(n)} = D_x \gamma^n G_n(\zeta, \theta), \qquad \text{......(22)}$$

where ζ has the value (20), and

$$\theta = -\frac{A+\delta}{\gamma}. \qquad \text{......(23)}$$

Putting, as usual, for the life-annuities

$$\mathrm{a}_x = \frac{1}{D_x} \sum_x^{\infty} D_x, \quad \bar{a}_x = \frac{1}{D_x} \int_x^{\infty} D_x dx,$$

the relation between a_x and $\bar{a}_x$ follows from Euler's summation formula† which, with infinity as upper limit of integration and summation, may be written

$$\int_0^{\infty} f(t)\, dt = \sum_0^{\infty} f(s) - \tfrac{1}{2} f(0) + \sum_{\nu=1}^{r-1} \frac{B_{2\nu}}{(2\nu)!} f^{(2\nu-1)}(0) + R, \text{...(24)}$$

$$R = \int_0^{\infty} \frac{\Delta_t \overline{B}_{2r}(0)}{(2r)!} f^{(2r)}(t)\, dt. \qquad \text{......(25)}$$

It is here assumed that $\int_0^{\infty} f(t)\, dt$ and $\sum_0^{\infty} f(s)$ are convergent, and that $f^{(2\nu-1)}(k) \to 0$ as $k \to \infty$ $(\nu = 1, 2, \ldots, r-1)$. The convergence of the remainder term follows from these conditions.

If we put $f(t) = D_{x+t}$, these conditions are clearly satisfied when the table of mortality is graduated by Makeham's formula.

* The actuarial function D_x must, of course, not be confounded with the symbol of differentiation employed above.

† *Interpolation*, § 14, formulas (9) and (10).

We thus obtain

$$\bar{a}_x = a_x - \tfrac{1}{2} + \sum_{\nu=1}^{r-1} \frac{B_{2\nu}}{(2\nu)!} \gamma^{2\nu-1} G_{2\nu-1}(\zeta, \theta) + R, \quad \ldots(26)$$

where $$R = \frac{\gamma^{2r}}{D_x} \int_0^\infty \frac{\Delta_t \overline{B}_{2r}(0)}{(2r)!} D_{x+t} G_{2r}(\zeta_{x+t}, \theta)\, dt. \quad \ldots\ldots(27)$$

In writing ζ_{x+t} instead of ζ we indicate that x has been replaced by $x+t$ in (20).

5. We may now by means of the inequality (18) find limits to the remainder term (27).

It follows from (21), (23) and (20) that we may choose the arbitrary constant k in (6), so that

$$D_x = \zeta^\theta e^{-\zeta}. \quad \ldots\ldots(28)$$

Inserting this in (27), noting that*

$$|\Delta_t \overline{B}_{2r}(0)| \leqslant (2 - 2^{1-2r}) |B_{2r}|, \quad \ldots\ldots(29)$$

we have

$$|R| < \gamma^{2r} \frac{2 - 2^{1-2r}}{(2r)!} |B_{2r}| \zeta^{-\theta} e^{\zeta} \int_x^\infty \zeta^\theta e^{-\zeta} |G_{2r}(\zeta, \theta)|\, dx;$$

or, as $dx = \dfrac{d\zeta}{\gamma\zeta}$, by (18), ζ being in our case positive and θ negative,

$$|R| < \gamma^{2r-1} \frac{2 - 2^{1-2r}}{(2r)!} |B_{2r}| \zeta^{-\theta} e^{\zeta} \int_\zeta^\infty \zeta^{\theta-1} e^{-\zeta} (\zeta - \theta + r - \tfrac{1}{2})^{2r}\, d\zeta. \quad \ldots\ldots(30)$$

But, by the Theorem of Mean Value,

$$\int_\zeta^\infty \zeta^{\theta-1} e^{-\zeta} (\zeta - \theta + r - \tfrac{1}{2})^{2r}\, d\zeta = e^{-\xi} (\xi - \theta + r - \tfrac{1}{2})^{2r} \int_\zeta^\infty \zeta^{\theta-1}\, d\zeta$$

$$= e^{-\xi} (\xi - \theta + r - \tfrac{1}{2})^{2r} \frac{\zeta^\theta}{|\theta|},$$

and the maximum value of $e^{-\xi} (\xi - \theta + r - \tfrac{1}{2})^{2r}$ is $(2r)^{2r} e^{-r-\theta-\frac{1}{2}}$. Hence

$$\int_\zeta^\infty \zeta^{\theta-1} e^{-\zeta} (\zeta - \theta + r - \tfrac{1}{2})^{2r}\, d\zeta < (2r)^{2r} e^{-r-\theta-\frac{1}{2}} \frac{\zeta^\theta}{|\theta|}.$$

Inserting this in (30) we have, finally,

$$|R| < \gamma^{2r-1} (2 - 2^{1-2r}) \frac{(2r)^{2r}}{(2r)!} \left| \frac{B_{2r}}{\theta} \right| e^{\zeta - r - \theta - \frac{1}{2}}. \quad \ldots\ldots(31)$$

* *Interpolation*, § 13, article 141 and formula (20).

6. As an application of (26) and (31), let us take $r = 3$. We then find

$$\bar{a}_x = a_x - \tfrac{1}{2} + \gamma\frac{\theta - \zeta}{12} - \gamma^3\frac{(\zeta-\theta)^2 - \zeta}{720} + R,$$

$$|R| < \frac{243}{80}\frac{\gamma^5}{|\theta|}e^{\zeta-\theta-3\cdot 5}.$$

The factor $\frac{243}{80}$ may be replaced by the slightly higher factor $\frac{10}{3}$, and for practical purposes it is preferable to put $-\theta = \kappa$, so that

$$\kappa = \frac{A + \delta}{\gamma}. \qquad \text{......(32)}$$

Further, we have, by (20) and (23),

$$\gamma\frac{\theta - \zeta}{12} = -\frac{\mu_x + \delta}{12}.$$

Finally, as the term $\gamma^3\frac{(\zeta-\theta)^2 - \zeta}{720}$ is generally very small, we include it in the remainder term, and write the formula*

$$\bar{a}_x = a_x - \tfrac{1}{2} - \frac{\mu_x + \delta}{12} + R, \qquad \text{......(33)}$$

$$|R| < \gamma^3\frac{(\zeta+\kappa)^2 + \zeta}{720} + \frac{10\gamma^5}{3\kappa}e^{\zeta+\kappa-3\cdot 5}. \qquad \text{......(34)}$$

It should be noted that the limits to the error given by (34) are, for the values occurring in practice, considerably closer than those obtained simply by putting $r = 2$ in (31), that is

$$|R| < \frac{2\gamma^3}{3\kappa}e^{\zeta+\kappa-2\cdot 5}.$$

The inequality (34) should, of course, not be applied in each individual case, but may with profit be employed for solving questions of a more general nature. For instance, it is of importance to know up to what age we may, for a given table, rely on the first three decimals of $\bar{a}_x$, calculated by (33). We must then, by trials, find the value of ζ for which the right-hand side of (34) equals ·0005. In the $O^{M(5)}$ table, to take an example, we have

$$A = \cdot 005888861, \quad \gamma = \cdot 08980082,$$

* An inequality of a similar character to (34) has been found by W. Friedli by a different method. See *Mitteilungen der Vereinigung schweizerischer Versicherungsmathematiker*, 13. Heft (1918), p. 267.

so that, at 4 per cent. interest, $\kappa = \cdot 50233$. As the first term in (34) is generally small in comparison with the second, we may begin by putting

$$\frac{10\gamma^5}{3\kappa} e^{\zeta+\kappa-3\cdot 5} = \cdot 0005,$$

whence $\zeta = 5\cdot 555$. This value is a little too large. Trying $\zeta = 5\cdot 4$, we get $|R| < \cdot 00047$, taking account of both terms in (34). This value of ζ corresponds to

$$\mu_x = \gamma\zeta + A = \cdot 4908,$$

or, as is seen by a glance at the table of μ_x, an age between 94 and 95.

The result is that if we calculate $\bar{a}_x$ by the usual approximate formula (33), we obtain at least three correct decimals in the result up to age 94, in the case of the $O^{M(5)}$ 4 per cent. table.

7. I shall not on this occasion go further into the question of numerical approximation, a subject which covers a considerable ground and cannot be adequately dealt with in a few lectures. But I think we may with profit cast a glance at certain simple *inequalities* which may often be of use to the actuary or statistician in their estimates. It is not yet sufficiently recognized that a considerable number of special results which have been derived by more or less heterogeneous methods, are all included, as particular cases, in simple inequalities of a very general and yet quite elementary nature. Such inequalities, between any number of functions, may often be derived by a very simple, almost intuitive, principle which I have frequently found useful*, and of which I proceed to make a novel application.

Let, for instance, $f(t)$ and $\phi(t)$ be two *positive* and *non-increasing* functions, and let $g(t)$ be a *positive* function. Then we have, if $\alpha \leqslant \mu \leqslant \beta$,

$$\frac{\sum_{\alpha}^{\mu} \phi(\nu) f(\nu) g(\nu)}{\sum_{\alpha}^{\mu} \phi(\nu) g(\nu)} \geqslant \frac{\sum_{\alpha}^{\beta} f(\nu) g(\nu)}{\sum_{\alpha}^{\beta} g(\nu)}; \qquad \ldots\ldots(35)$$

for both sides of this inequality represent weighted means of $f(\nu)$, but on the left, larger weights have been attributed to the larger values of $f(\nu)$, as the values left out, or $f(\mu+1)$, $f(\mu+2)$, ... $f(\beta)$, may be considered as included with infinitely small weights.

* See, for instance, *The Journal of the Institute of Actuaries*, vol. LI, pp. 274–275.

As a rule the sign $\geqslant$ in (35) may be replaced by $>$, as equality only occurs in certain limiting cases, for instance when $\phi(t)$ is a constant and $\mu = \beta$, or when $f(\nu)$ is a constant.

A similar inequality holds for integrals; let $f(t)$, $\phi(t)$ and $g(t)$ have the same properties as before, and let $a \leqslant \tau \leqslant b$; then

$$\frac{\int_a^\tau \phi(t) f(t) g(t)\, dt}{\int_a^\tau \phi(t) g(t)\, dt} \geqslant \frac{\int_a^b f(t) g(t)\, dt}{\int_a^b g(t)\, dt}. \quad \text{......(36)}$$

This inequality may be established independently by a similar reasoning, or may be looked upon as a limiting case of (35).

The proof we have given of (35) is really intuitive; but it is easy to give an arithmetical proof. Nothing prevents us from putting $\phi(\mu + 1)$, $\phi(\mu + 2)$, ... $\phi(\beta)$ equal to zero and taking the limits of summation as α and β everywhere. We then have to prove that the difference

$$\sum_\alpha^\beta \phi(\nu) f(\nu) g(\nu) \,.\, \sum_\alpha^\beta g(\nu) - \sum_\alpha^\beta \phi(\nu) g(\nu) \,.\, \sum_\alpha^\beta f(\nu) g(\nu)$$

cannot be negative. Performing the multiplications, we get terms of the form

$$\phi(n) f(n) g(n) \,.\, g(m) - \phi(n) g(n) \,.\, f(m) g(m)$$

which vanish if $n = m$. If $n \neq m$, we may assume $n < m$ and add another term, where n and m have been exchanged. We then have to prove that the expression

$$\left.\begin{aligned} &\phi(n) f(n) g(n) \,.\, g(m) + \phi(m) f(m) g(m) \,.\, g(n) \\ &- \phi(n) g(n) \,.\, f(m) g(m) - \phi(m) g(m) \,.\, f(n) g(n) \end{aligned}\right\}$$

cannot be negative. But this expression can be written in the form

$$g(n) g(m) [f(n) - f(m)] [\phi(n) - \phi(m)]$$

which, as $n < m$, cannot assume negative values.

Simple, as the inequalities (35) and (36) are, they are by no means trivial. Thus, putting $g(\nu) = 1$, $\mu = \beta$, we obtain from (35) Tchebychef's celebrated inequality

$$\sum_\alpha^\beta \phi(\nu) f(\nu) \geqslant \frac{1}{\beta - \alpha + 1} \sum_\alpha^\beta \phi(\nu) \,.\, \sum_\alpha^\beta f(\nu), \quad \text{......(37)}$$

and from (36), putting $g(t) = 1$, $\tau = b$, the corresponding inequality for integrals

$$\int_a^b \phi(t) f(t)\, dt \geqslant \frac{1}{b - a} \int_a^b \phi(t)\, dt \,.\, \int_a^b f(t)\, dt, \quad \text{......(38)}$$

both of which are valid if ϕ and f are positive and non-increasing functions.

The inequalities (35) and (36) are closely related to certain other inequalities*, and it may be proved that they hold on assumptions which are less restricted than those made here. I believe, however, that the forms suggested above are preferable from a practical point of view, because the intuitive principle by which they are obtained makes it easy to derive them and, besides, lends itself to generalizations, e.g. by introducing more functions.

8. Turning our attention to the applications, we shall first, in (36), put $f(t) = b^r - t^r$, assuming $r > 0$ and $0 \leqslant a < b$. We then get

$$\frac{\int_a^b t^r g(t)\,dt}{\int_a^b g(t)\,dt} \geqslant \frac{\int_a^\tau t^r g(t)\,\phi(t)\,dt}{\int_a^\tau g(t)\,\phi(t)\,dt}. \qquad \ldots\ldots(39)$$

This is an inequality between *moments* which is sometimes useful. Thus, putting $a = 0$, $b = \infty$, $\tau = \infty$, $r = 1$, $g(t) = -l'_{x+t}$, we find

$$\frac{\int_0^\infty t l'_{x+t}\,dt}{\int_0^\infty l'_{x+t}\,dt} \geqslant \frac{\int_0^\infty t l'_{x+t}\,\phi(t)\,dt}{\int_0^\infty l'_{x+t}\,\phi(t)\,dt}$$

or

$$\bar{e}_x \geqslant \frac{\int_0^\infty t\mu_{x+t}\,l_{x+t}\,\phi(t)\,dt}{\int_0^\infty \mu_{x+t}\,l_{x+t}\,\phi(t)\,dt}.$$

Now, if μ_{x+t} does not decrease for $t > 0$, we may put $\phi(t) = \dfrac{1}{\mu_{x+t}}$ and thus obtain

$$\bar{e}_x \geqslant \frac{\int_0^\infty t l_{x+t}\,dt}{\int_0^\infty l_{x+t}\,dt}$$

or

$$x + \bar{e}_x \geqslant \frac{\int_x^\infty x l_x\,dx}{\int_x^\infty l_x\,dx}, \qquad \ldots\ldots(40)$$

provided only that μ_x *does not decrease* for increasing x.

* *Skandinavisk Aktuarietidskrift* (1925), p. 137.

This formula has been proved by different methods and on various assumptions as to the mortality table by L. v. Bortkiewicz*, K. Pearson† and E. J. Gumbel‡. I have shown elsewhere§ that the condition $\mu_{x+t} \geqslant \mu_x$ for $t \geqslant 0$, may be replaced by the less restricted condition $\bar{e}_{x+t} \leqslant \bar{e}_x$ for $t \geqslant 0$.

More generally, we find, putting $a = 0$, $b = \infty$, $\tau = \infty$, $g(t) = -D'_{x+t}$, $\phi(t) = \dfrac{1}{\mu_{x+t} + \delta}$,

$$\int_0^\infty t^r D_{x+t} dt \leqslant r\bar{a}_x \int_0^\infty t^{r-1} D_{x+t} dt, \qquad \text{......(41)}$$

which may also be written

$$I^r \bar{a}_x \leqslant \bar{a}_x \, . \, I^{r-1} \bar{a}_x, \qquad \text{......(42)}$$

denoting by $I^r \bar{a}_x$ the annuity of order $r+1$,

$$I^r \bar{a}_x = \frac{1}{r!\, D_x} \int_0^\infty t^r D_{x+t} dt. \qquad \text{......(43)}$$

By repeated application of (42) we get

$$I^r \bar{a}_x \leqslant \bar{a}_x^{\,r+1}. \qquad \text{......(44)}$$

These results may be used for finding limits to the remainder term if we calculate the annuity-value at a different force of interest by developing in powers of the difference between the two forces of interest.

Corresponding results may be obtained from (35) in the discontinuous case.

9. Further, let i_1 be a rate of interest greater than i, and let us put

$$f(\nu) = \left(\frac{1+i}{1+i_1}\right)^\nu, \; g(\nu) = \frac{1}{(1+i)^\nu}, \; \phi(\nu) = l_{x+\nu}, \; \alpha = 1, \; \beta = \mu = n.$$

We then obtain, by (35), a result which may be written

$$\frac{a^1_{x\overline{n}|}}{a^1_{\overline{n}|}} > \frac{a_{x\overline{n}|}}{a_{\overline{n}|}} \qquad (i_1 > i), \qquad \text{......(45)}$$

where $a^1_{x\overline{n}|}$ denotes the temporary life-annuity, $a^1_{\overline{n}|}$ the annuity-certain, at the rate of interest i_1.

* *Die mittlere Lebensdauer*, Jena, 1893, p. 77.
† *Biometrika*, vol. XVI, p. 297.
‡ *Ibid.* vol. XVII, p. 173.
§ L.c. p. 145.

If, on the other hand, we put

$$\phi(\nu) = l_{x+\nu},\ f(\nu) = l_{y+\nu},\ g(\nu) = (1+i)^{-\nu},\ \alpha = 1,\ \beta = \mu = n,$$

we find
$$\frac{a_{xy\overline{n}|}}{a_{y\overline{n}|}} \geqslant \frac{a_{x\overline{n}|}}{a_{\overline{n}|}}. \qquad \text{......(46)}$$

This kind of result may be varied in many ways, for instance by introducing more lives, by considering continuous annuity values, etc.

10. As another example of the application of our inequalities, let us consider the policy value of an endowment assurance. If the sum insured is unity, the age at entry x, the original duration n, then the value of the policy after t years is*

$$V = 1 - \frac{\mathrm{a}_{x+t:\overline{n-t}|}}{\mathrm{a}_{x\overline{n}|}}, \qquad \text{......(47)}$$

where $\mathrm{a}_{x\overline{n}|}$ denotes the temporary life annuity-due. It is assumed in this formula that the premiums are annual, and that the sum insured becomes payable at the end of the policy year of death, or at the expiration of n years if the person insured be then alive.

Now let V_1 be the corresponding policy value at the rate of interest i_1. It is, then, easy to prove that V_1 cannot be smaller than V, if $i_1 < i$, that is

$$V \leqslant V_1 \qquad (i_1 < i), \qquad \text{......(48)}$$

provided only that μ_x *does not decrease* for increasing x.

For if this condition is satisfied, the function $\phi(\nu) = \dfrac{l_{x+\nu+t}}{l_{x+\nu}}$ is a non-increasing function, as is seen on examining $\phi'(\nu)$. If we put, further,

$$g(\nu) = (1+i_1)^{-\nu}\, l_{x+\nu},\quad f(\nu) = \left(\frac{1+i_1}{1+i}\right)^{\nu}$$

and $\alpha = 0$, $\beta = n-1$, $\mu = n-t-1$, all the conditions assumed in (35) are satisfied, and we find

$$\frac{\mathrm{a}_{x+t:\overline{n-t}|}}{\mathrm{a}^{\mathrm{I}}_{x+t:\overline{n-t}|}} \geqslant \frac{\mathrm{a}_{x\overline{n}|}}{\mathrm{a}^{\mathrm{I}}_{x\overline{n}|}},$$

which is the same thing as (48).

In a similar way we obtain from (36), on the same condition as regards μ_x, and denoting by $\overline{V}$ the policy value in the case of continuous payment,

$$\overline{V} \leqslant \overline{V}_1 \qquad (\delta_1 < \delta). \qquad \text{......(49)}$$

* *Institute of Actuaries' Text-Book*, Part II, Second Ed. (1902), p. 351.

11. As a last application of (35), let us consider the free, or paid-up, policy that can be granted in the case of a pure endowment with annual premiums, if the payment of premiums is discontinued after t years.

Let the age at entry be x, the term of the endowment n, and let the premium be payable for r years. Then the free policy per unit is, after t years*

$$W = \frac{\sum_{x}^{x+t-1} D_x}{\sum_{x}^{x+r-1} D_x} \qquad (t \leqslant r \leqslant n). \qquad \ldots\ldots(50)$$

In practice, this free policy is sometimes calculated as $\frac{t}{r}$, an irrational rule which, besides simplicity, has the only (doubtful) advantage that the policy-holders imagine that they understand it. On the other hand, it is safe to use from the point of view of the company, as it can be proved by (35) that the resulting value cannot exceed the correct value, that is

$$W \geqslant \frac{t}{r}. \qquad \ldots\ldots(51)$$

For this result follows immediately from (35), putting

$$\phi(\nu) = g(\nu) = 1, \ f(\nu) = D_{x+\nu}, \ \alpha = 0, \ \mu = t - 1, \ \beta = r - 1.$$

* *Text-Book*, p. 356.

Third Lecture

1. In this last lecture I shall deal with the theoretical foundation of certain types of frequency-functions.

If a statistical variable x can assume certain values x_i with the corresponding probabilities $f(x_i)$, then $f(x)$ is called the frequency-function of the argument x. Assuming the arguments x_i to be distinct, $f(x)$ is a *discontinuous* frequency-function.

But there are cases where the statistical variable can assume any value belonging to a certain interval. If, in that case, there exists a function $f(x)$ such that $f(x)\,dx$ is the probability of a result situated between x and $x + dx$, we call $f(x)$ a *continuous* frequency-function of the argument x.

Cases may of course be imagined where x can assume any value belonging to a certain interval and, besides, certain isolated values; but as such cases are of no practical importance, we confine our attention to the two main classes, the discontinuous and the continuous frequency-function.

The definition itself tells us very little about the nature of $f(x)$. It tells us, in fact, only that $f(x)$ must be positive, and that, in the discontinuous case, $\Sigma f(x) = 1$, in the continuous case $\int f(x)\,dx = 1$, the summation, or integration, being extended to the whole field of possible values of x.

But in our search for suitable types of frequency-functions we are greatly aided by the consideration that, according to the above definition, a frequency-function (in the continuous case after multiplication by dx) is nothing but a *probability considered as a function of a parameter*. It is the lasting merit of Professor Karl Pearson of the University of London to have pointed out convincingly that the *natural source* of practically useful types of frequency-functions is the elementary calculus of probabilities. What nature does in producing a new individual, practically comes to the same thing as drawing from various urns and mixing up the results. This explains the great success of Pearson's types. Hence we may also as a general rule presume that a *product* of elementary probabilities is more likely to yield a practically useful frequency-function than a *sum* of such probabilities.

As an example of what I have in view, let us derive Pearson's *First Main Type* (Type I) by the method which seems to me the most convincing one*.

Let us assume that three numbers a, x and b are given,

* The names "Main Type" and "Transition Type" seem due to Mr W. Palin Elderton; see *Frequency-Curves and Correlation*, Second Ed. pp. 42–43.

$a < x < b$, and that we are making experiments, the results of which are confined to the interval from a to b in such a way that all results between these limits are equally likely to occur. It is very easy to realize these conditions in practice: we may, for instance, let the interval $b - a$ be represented by the circumference of a roulette on which the length $x - a$ has been marked off. The probability of a result between a and x is, then, $\frac{x-a}{b-a}$, and the probability of a result between x and b is $\frac{b-x}{b-a}$, together unity.

Let us now make a *compound experiment*, consisting of k individual experiments. The probability of obtaining ν results between a and x, and the remainder between x and b, is

$$\binom{k}{\nu}\left(\frac{x-a}{b-a}\right)^{\nu}\left(\frac{b-x}{b-a}\right)^{k-\nu}.$$

If we add one more experiment to the compound experiment, demanding that one of the $k + 1$ results shall fall between x and $x + dx$, and the remaining k as before, the above probability must be multiplied by $(k+1)\frac{dx}{b-a}$, as the last added result can occur at any of the $k + 1$ places in the sequence.

The probability of the compound result is, therefore,

$$f(x)\,dx = \binom{k}{\nu}\frac{k+1}{b-a}\left(\frac{x-a}{b-a}\right)^{\nu}\left(\frac{b-x}{b-a}\right)^{k-\nu} dx,$$

whence, if we write for abbreviation

$$H = \binom{k}{\nu}\frac{k+1}{(b-a)^{k+1}}, \qquad \text{......(1)}$$

Pearson's First Main Type

$$f(x) = H(x-a)^{\nu}(b-x)^{k-\nu} \qquad (a \leqslant x \leqslant b). \text{ ......(2)}$$

If we look upon a, b, k and ν as constants characterizing the compound observation, it is easy to indicate what must be considered as the observed value of the variable x. We make a compound experiment consisting of $k + 1$ individual experiments, the results of which we set off on the line from a to b. The observed value of x is, then, the $(\nu + 1)$th point from the left.

We have derived Pearson's First Main Type on the assumption that k and ν are integers. The extension to non-integral, positive values of k and ν does not present any serious difficulty, as it is really only a question of interpolating between frequency-functions with integral values of these constants. In this case, the binomial factor $\binom{k}{\nu}$ is, of course, interpreted by Gamma-functions.

Pearson's *Third Main Type* (Type VI) is nothing but (2), interpreted differently, and is obtained if we take b instead of x as variable and determine the constant factor so that the total probability is unity. We need not go into details.

But it seems more difficult to connect Pearson's *Second Main Type* (Type IV) with elementary probabilities. If we put

$$\left.\begin{aligned} a &= \alpha + \beta\sqrt{-1} \\ b &= \alpha - \beta\sqrt{-1} \end{aligned}\right\} \qquad \left.\begin{aligned} \nu &= -\gamma + \tfrac{1}{2}\lambda\sqrt{-1} \\ k - \nu &= -\gamma - \tfrac{1}{2}\lambda\sqrt{-1} \end{aligned}\right\} \quad \ldots\ldots(3)$$

we obtain from (2) Pearson's Second Main Type

$$f(x) = K\left[1 + \left(\frac{x-\alpha}{\beta}\right)^2\right]^{-\gamma} e^{-\lambda \operatorname{arc} tg \frac{x-\alpha}{\beta}}. \quad \ldots\ldots(4)$$

From a purely mathematical point of view the introduction of this type is, therefore, quite natural and simple. But the connection with experimental facts is lost by thus admitting complex values of constants which were assumed to be real. It is easy by means of a roulette arrangement to illustrate the probabilities

$$p \equiv \frac{1}{2\pi} \operatorname{arc} tg \frac{x-\alpha}{\beta} \quad \text{and} \quad dp = \frac{1}{1 + \left(\frac{x-\alpha}{\beta}\right)^2} \cdot \frac{dx}{2\pi\beta};$$

and (4) may be built up by means of these probabilities; but this proceeding seems too artificial to carry conviction, and I hope that someone will be able to make a better suggestion.

2. To expatiate, on this occasion, on the work of the English School of biometricians founded and headed by Karl Pearson would, however, be "carrying coals to Newcastle." The chief object of this lecture is to deal with the point of view of the Continental School, a subject towards which I confess that I feel less attracted, but on which I have, nevertheless, more to say.

A number of continental writers, amongst them Thiele, Bruns and Charlier, while in England Edgeworth has represented a similar point of view, look upon the question of describing statistical distributions as a question of *development in a series*. In physics, trigonometric series are often used with remarkable success for developing functions of a more or less unknown nature. Why not attempt a similar thing in statistics? But as, in the case of frequency-distributions, cos nx and sin nx do not look very promising as elements in such series, search must be made for more suitable elements. Several authors—I leave aside all questions of priority—have proposed that we should use the *derivatives* of the Gaussian or "normal" error-function. Series of this form, that is

$$f(x) = \sum_{n=0}^{\infty} a_n D_x^n e^{-\frac{(x-\lambda)^2}{2\kappa^2}}, \qquad \text{......(5)}$$

are usually called *A*-series.

For cases presenting an exceptional degree of skewness, Charlier has proposed another series, proceeding by *differences* of Poisson's frequency-function. This function is originally only defined for *non-negative, integral* values of the argument ν, viz.

$$\psi(\nu) = \frac{\kappa^\nu e^{-\kappa}}{\nu!} \qquad (\nu \geqslant 0). \qquad \text{......(6)}$$

But from this, Charlier constructs a continuous function $\psi(x)$, defined for all, positive or negative, values of x, putting

$$\psi(x) = \frac{e^{-\kappa}}{\pi}\int_0^\pi e^{\kappa \cos t} \cos(\kappa \sin t - xt)\, dt. \qquad \text{......(7)}$$

It is easily verified that for $x = \nu$, $\psi(x)$ assumes the values (6)*.

If, now, ∇ denotes the ascending difference, that is

$$\nabla\psi(x) = \psi(x) - \psi(x-1),$$

Charlier puts

$$f(x) = \sum_{n=0}^{\infty} b_n \nabla^n \psi(x), \qquad \text{......(8)}$$

which is his so-called *B*-series.

The question naturally presents itself, under what circumstances the *A*- and *B*-series may reasonably be said to represent frequency-distributions. For it is perfectly clear that the series (5) and (8) as they stand, with an infinity of terms, need have nothing whatever to do with frequency-distributions, any more than a trigonometric series need represent a function with properties similar to those of its individual terms. They are

* Writing $i = \sqrt{-1}$, we have, as the imaginary part vanishes,

$$\psi(x) = \frac{e^{-\kappa}}{2\pi}\int_{-\pi}^{\pi} e^{\kappa e^{it} - ixt}\, dt$$

$$= \frac{e^{-\kappa}\sin \pi x}{\pi}\sum_{n=0}^{\infty}(-1)^n \frac{\kappa^n}{n!\,(x-n)}.$$

simply series representing more or less general classes of functions. Whether such expressions as (5) and (8) deserve the name of "frequency-functions" depends entirely on whether they may be interpreted as probabilities or not.

We are therefore of opinion that the labour that has been expended by several authors in examining the conditions under which the A-series is ultimately convergent, interesting as it is from the point of view of mathematical analysis, has no bearing on the question of the statistical applications. What we want to know is, whether the first three or four terms of the series can be looked upon as a frequency-function, in which case we are also sure that our function only depends on a limited number of constants to be determined by the experience. That an expression containing an unlimited number of constants can be made to fit a limited experience, is neither surprising nor interesting.

There are other drawbacks to development in an infinite series. If, as is usually the case, the coefficients are determined by the method of moments, the validity of inverting the order in which the summations or integrations are performed must be proved. This difficulty does not exist, if we look at the problem merely as a *question of graduation* by means of a formula containing a *finite* number of constants. But then, as in all questions of graduation, it becomes imperative to have good reasons to believe that the formula chosen will fit the observations. And this means, in our case, first of all that the formula must represent a *probability*.

There is a special objection to the use of the *continuous* function $\psi(x)$ introduced by Charlier, and that is that the moments of $\psi(x)$ taken between the limits $\pm\infty$ are *divergent*, as I have shown elsewhere*. It seems altogether unnatural to generalize $\psi(\nu)$ as defined by (6) into the continuous function (7), defined for all real values of x. While $\psi(\nu)$ is a well-defined probability, $\psi(x)$ cannot generally be interpreted as a probability, as for small values of κ, $\psi(x)$ approaches to $\frac{\sin \pi x}{\pi x}$ which can assume negative values.

3. I shall now, avoiding the use of infinite series, proceed to investigate under what circumstances a *finite* number of terms of an A-series or a B-series may be looked upon as a frequency-function, i.e. a probability, and how the constants may be determined by the method of moments. I take the terms "A-series" and "B-series" in a somewhat extended sense, meaning by an

* *Svenska Aktuarieföreningens Tidskrift* (1916), pp. 226–228.

"*A*-series" a series that proceeds by differential coefficients, and by a "*B*-series" a series that proceeds by differences, of a given frequency-function *which I shall not specify*. Only it must be understood that the frequency-function thus employed as generating element must be a genuine frequency-function of an elementary type, that is*, a probability depending on a parameter, so that its value is always positive (or zero). I have, in fact, dealt with this question before†, but from a less general point of view, having observed later on that it is possible to treat the *A*-series and *B*-series simultaneously.

Let the generating function be $\phi(x)$. This function may, according to circumstances, be a discontinuous frequency-function, such as the binomial function, Poisson's function, etc.; or it may be a continuous frequency-function, such as the Gaussian function, one of Pearson's types, etc.

It is then clear that the expression

$$f(x) = \sum_{\nu=0}^{k} A_\nu \phi(x - \nu\omega), \qquad \ldots\ldots(9)$$

where

$$\sum_{\nu=0}^{k} A_\nu = 1, \qquad \ldots\ldots(10)$$

is a frequency-function, provided only that the constants A_ν, without being necessarily all positive, are such that $f(x)$ does not assume negative values. For it follows from (10) that‡ $\Sigma f(x) = 1$ in the case of discontinuous functions, and $\int f(x)\,dx = 1$ in the case of continuous functions. And a linear function of probabilities may, under these circumstances, evidently always be interpreted as a probability.

4. Before continuing, it will be suitable to recapitulate the notation which will be used as regards moments and similar functions.

If there are n repeated experiments or observations o_i, we write, as in the First Lecture,

$$\sigma_r = \frac{1}{n} \sum_{i=1}^{n} o_i^r. \qquad \ldots\ldots(11)$$

* If continuous, after multiplication by dx.

† On Charlier's Generalized Frequency-Function. *Skandinavisk Aktuarietidskrift* (1924), pp. 147–152.

‡ In leaving out the limits of summation and integration we indicate that the summation or integration is extended to the whole range of existence of the frequency-function. This range may always be taken as $\pm\infty$, if the frequency-function is defined as zero outside the range for which it is employed, a very convenient convention. It is possible to include sums and integrals in one formula, but only by modifying the usual definition of an integral in a way with which the actuarial world is not yet familiar (Stieltjes' Integral) and which we would therefore rather avoid.

The corresponding true values are, according to circumstances, calculated as

$$\bar{\sigma}_r = \Sigma x^r f(x) \quad \text{or} \quad \bar{\sigma}_r = \int x^r f(x)\,dx. \qquad \ldots\ldots(12)$$

It is, of course, assumed that the nature of the function $\phi(x)$, used for representing $f(x)$ as shown in (9), is such that the moments (12), up to the order actually employed, are convergent.

The moments (about the origin) belonging to $\phi(x)$ will be denoted by σ_r', that is

$$\sigma_r' = \Sigma x^r \phi(x) \quad \text{or} \quad \sigma_r' = \int x^r \phi(x)\,dx \qquad \ldots\ldots(13)$$

according to circumstances.

Finally, it will be convenient to introduce the notation

$$\sigma_r'' = \sum_{\nu=0}^{k} \nu^r A_\nu, \qquad \ldots\ldots(14)$$

although A_ν is not a frequency-function, but may assume negative values, so that there is only a formal analogy with $\bar{\sigma}_r$ and σ_r'.

The different kinds of moments about the origin having been thus defined, it is hardly necessary to explain what must be understood by the corresponding moments about the mean, semi-invariants, etc. For instance, the relation connecting the semi-invariants with the moments about the mean, that is

$$\sigma_{r+1} = \sum_{\nu=0}^{r} \binom{r}{\nu} \mu_{\nu+1}\, \sigma_{r-\nu}, \qquad \ldots\ldots(15)$$

also holds if we replace σ and μ by $\bar{\sigma}$ and $\bar{\mu}$, by σ' and μ', or by σ'' and μ''. The same applies to the relation

$$e^{\frac{\mu_1}{1!}t + \frac{\mu_2}{2!}t^2 + \ldots} = 1 + \frac{\sigma_1}{1!}t + \frac{\sigma_2}{2!}t^2 + \ldots, \qquad \ldots\ldots(16)$$

which is equivalent with (15).

A few words are advisable about the *factorial moments**, an interesting class of functions which have not yet come into such general use as they deserve. The rth factorial moment is denoted by $\sigma_{(r)}$ and defined by

$$\left.\begin{aligned} \sigma_{(r)} &= \frac{1}{n}\sum_{i=1}^{n} o_i(o_i-1)\ldots(o_i-r+1) \\ &= \frac{1}{n}\sum_{i=1}^{n} o_i^{(r)} \end{aligned}\right\}. \qquad \ldots\ldots(17)$$

* These functions are, in principle, already found in W. Palin Elderton's *Frequency-Curves and Correlation* (1906), p. 20, or (1927) p. 20. A more systematic treatment of them is due to W. F. Sheppard, see his paper "Factorial Moments in Terms of Sums or Differences" (*Proc. of the London Math. Soc.* Ser. 2, vol. XIII, Part 2). The notation used below is that of my paper "Factorial Moments and Discontinuous Frequency-Functions" (*Skandinavisk Aktuarietidskrift*, 1923, p. 73).

As*

$$x^{(r)} = \sum_{\nu=0}^{r} x^{\nu} \frac{D^{\nu} 0^{(r)}}{\nu!},$$

we have

$$\sigma_{(r)} = \sum_{\nu=0}^{r} \sigma_{\nu} \frac{D^{\nu} 0^{(r)}}{\nu!}; \qquad \text{......(18)}$$

and inversely, from

$$x^{r} = \sum_{\nu=0}^{r} x^{(\nu)} \frac{\Delta^{\nu} 0^{r}}{\nu!},$$

we find

$$\sigma_{r} = \sum_{\nu=0}^{r} \sigma_{(\nu)} \frac{\Delta^{\nu} 0^{r}}{\nu!}, \qquad \text{......(19)}$$

so that the functions $\sigma_{(r)}$ and σ_r are equivalent†.

The relations (18) and (19) evidently hold, if σ is replaced by $\bar{\sigma}$, σ' or σ''. The function $\bar{\sigma}_{(r)}$ is defined by

$$\bar{\sigma}_{(r)} = \Sigma\, x^{(r)} f(x) \quad \text{or} \quad \bar{\sigma}_{(r)} = \int x^{(r)} f(x)\, dx, \qquad \text{......(20)}$$

while, in the case of $\sigma_{(r)}'$, $\phi(x)$ takes the place of $f(x)$. For $\sigma_{(r)}''$ we have

$$\sigma_{(r)}'' = \sum_{\nu=r}^{k} \nu^{(r)} A_{\nu}. \qquad \text{......(21)}$$

The factorial moments about the mean are denoted by $m_{(r)}$ and defined by

$$m_{(r)} = \frac{1}{n} \sum_{i=1}^{n} (o_i - m_1)^{(r)} \quad (r > 1), \qquad \text{......(22)}$$

while $m_{(1)} = m_1$. Developing the right-hand side in powers of $(o_i - m_1)$, we have

$$m_{(r)} = \sum_{\nu=2}^{r} m_{\nu} \frac{D^{\nu} 0^{(r)}}{\nu!} \quad (r > 1). \qquad \text{......(23)}$$

The functions $m_{(r)}$, m_r, σ_r, etc., are thus equivalent.

The relation (23) evidently holds, if m is replaced by $\bar{m}$, m' or m''.

The functions $\bar{\sigma}_r$, σ_r' and σ_r'' are connected by an important relation which may be obtained as follows. Let us, for instance, assume that the frequency-function is continuous, (the same argument may be followed step by step, if it is discontinuous); we have, then,

$$\bar{\sigma}_r = \int x^r f(x)\, dx$$

$$= \sum_{\nu=0}^{k} A_{\nu} \int x^r \phi(x - \nu\omega)\, dx;$$

* *Interpolation*, § 6.

† Tables of the coefficients in (18) and (19) are, for instance, found in *Interpolation*, § 6.

but, by the binomial theorem,

$$x^r = \sum_{s=0}^{r} \binom{r}{s} (x - \nu\omega)^s (\nu\omega)^{r-s};$$

hence $\bar{\sigma}_r = \sum_{\nu=0}^{k} A_\nu \sum_{s=0}^{r} \binom{r}{s} (\nu\omega)^{r-s} \int (x - \nu\omega)^s \phi(x - \nu\omega)\, dx$

$$= \sum_{\nu=0}^{k} A_\nu \sum_{s=0}^{r} \binom{r}{s} (\nu\omega)^{r-s} \sigma_s'$$

$$= \sum_{s=0}^{r} \binom{r}{s} \omega^{r-s} \sigma_s' \sum_{\nu=0}^{k} A_\nu \nu^{r-s};$$

or

$$\bar{\sigma}_r = \sum_{s=0}^{r} \binom{r}{s} \omega^{r-s} \sigma_s' \sigma_{r-s}'', \qquad \text{......(24)}$$

valid both for continuous and discontinuous frequency-functions.

Although this relation is quite simple, it is often more advantageous to employ the still simpler relation between the corresponding semi-invariants, or

$$\bar{\mu}_r = \mu_r' + \omega^r \mu_r''. \qquad \text{......(25)}$$

In order to obtain this, we multiply the relation

$$e^{\frac{\mu_1'}{1!}t + \frac{\mu_2'}{2!}t^2 + \dots} = 1 + \frac{\sigma_1'}{1!}t + \frac{\sigma_2'}{2!}t^2 + \dots$$

by the relation

$$e^{\frac{\mu_1''}{1!}\omega t + \frac{\mu_2''}{2!}\omega^2 t^2 + \dots} = 1 + \frac{\sigma_1''}{1!}\omega t + \frac{\sigma_2''}{2!}\omega^2 t^2 + \dots.$$

The coefficient of t^r in the exponent on the left then becomes

$$\frac{1}{r!}(\mu_r' + \omega^r \mu_r''),$$

while the coefficient of t^r on the right becomes

$$\frac{\sigma_r''}{r!}\omega^r + \frac{\sigma_{r-1}''}{(r-1)!}\frac{\sigma_1'}{1!}\omega^{r-1} + \dots + \frac{\sigma_r'}{r!} = \frac{\bar{\sigma}_r}{r!}.$$

As

$$e^{\frac{\bar{\mu}_1}{1!}t + \frac{\bar{\mu}_2}{2!}t^2 + \dots} = 1 + \frac{\bar{\sigma}_1}{1!}t + \frac{\bar{\sigma}_2}{2!}t^2 + \dots,$$

we therefore have

$$\frac{\bar{\mu}_r}{r!} = \frac{1}{r!}(\mu_r' + \omega^r \mu_r'')$$

or (25).

5. After these preliminaries we proceed to transform the frequency-function $f(x)$, defined by (9).

Making use of the operators* E^a and $\underset{\omega}{\nabla}$ defined by

$$E^a F(x) = F(x+a), \qquad \underset{\omega}{\nabla} F(x) = \frac{F(x) - F(x-\omega)}{\omega},$$

so that $$\underset{\omega}{\nabla} = \frac{1 - E^{-\omega}}{\omega}, \qquad E^{-\omega} = 1 - \omega \underset{\omega}{\nabla}, \qquad \text{......(26)}$$

we have

$$\phi(x - \nu\omega) = E^{-\nu\omega} \phi(x) = (1 - \omega \underset{\omega}{\nabla})^\nu \phi(x);$$

or, developing the binomial,

$$\phi(x - \nu\omega) = \sum_{s=0}^{\nu} (-1)^s \binom{\nu}{s} \omega^s \underset{\omega}{\nabla}^s \phi(x). \qquad \text{......(27)}$$

Inserting this in (9), we have

$$f(x) = \sum_{\nu=0}^{k} A_\nu \sum_{s=0}^{\nu} (-1)^s \binom{\nu}{s} \omega^s \underset{\omega}{\nabla}^s \phi(x).$$

As $\binom{\nu}{s}$ vanishes for $s > \nu$, we may write $\sum_{s=0}^{k}$ instead of $\sum_{s=0}^{\nu}$ and then, changing the order of summation, we obtain

$$f(x) = \sum_{s=0}^{k} \frac{(-1)^s}{s!} \omega^s \underset{\omega}{\nabla}^s \phi(x) \sum_{\nu=0}^{k} \nu^{(s)} A_\nu.$$

But $$\sum_{\nu=0}^{k} \nu^{(s)} A_\nu = \sum_{\nu=s}^{k} \nu^{(s)} A_\nu = \sigma_{(s)}'',$$

so that finally

$$f(x) = \sum_{s=0}^{k} \frac{(-1)^s}{s!} \omega^s \sigma_{(s)}'' \underset{\omega}{\nabla}^s \phi(x). \qquad \text{......(28)}$$

In order to represent a frequency-distribution by this formula, we first calculate the $\bar{\mu}_r$ which are obtained approximately from the observations, as mentioned in the First Lecture. Next, the μ_r' are calculated by means of the given function $\phi(x)$. We may then calculate the μ_r'' by the formula

$$\mu_r'' = \frac{\bar{\mu}_r - \mu_r'}{\omega^r}, \qquad \text{......(29)}$$

resulting from (25), and finally the $\sigma_{(r)}''$ which are obtained

* For the elements of the Calculus of Symbols we may, for instance, refer to Steffensen, *Interpolation*, §§ 2 and 18.

from the μ_r'' by the same formulas which connect the $\sigma_{(r)}$ with the μ_r, that is (15) and (18), or

$$\left.\begin{aligned} \sigma_1 &= \mu_1 \\ \sigma_2 &= \mu_1\sigma_1 + \mu_2 \\ \sigma_3 &= \mu_1\sigma_2 + 2\mu_2\sigma_1 + \mu_3 \\ \sigma_4 &= \mu_1\sigma_3 + 3\mu_2\sigma_2 + 3\mu_3\sigma_1 + \mu_4 \\ &\ldots\ldots\ldots\ldots\ldots\ldots \end{aligned}\right\} \qquad \ldots\ldots(30)$$

and

$$\left.\begin{aligned} \sigma_{(1)} &= \sigma_1 \\ \sigma_{(2)} &= \sigma_2 - \sigma_1 \\ \sigma_{(3)} &= \sigma_3 - 3\sigma_2 + 2\sigma_1 \\ \sigma_{(4)} &= \sigma_4 - 6\sigma_3 + 11\sigma_2 - 6\sigma_1 \\ &\ldots\ldots\ldots\ldots\ldots\ldots \end{aligned}\right\}. \qquad \ldots\ldots(31)$$

6. The frequency-function (28) is evidently nothing but the first $k+1$ terms of a generalized *B*-series

$$\sum_{s=0}^{\infty} c_s \underset{\omega}{\nabla^s} \phi(x). \qquad \ldots\ldots(32)$$

We have found the *necessary and sufficient conditions* which must be satisfied in order that the first $k+1$ terms of (32),

$$f(x) = \sum_{s=0}^{k} c_s \underset{\omega}{\nabla^s} \phi(x), \qquad \ldots\ldots(33)$$

shall be a frequency-function. These conditions are that $f(x)$ does not assume negative values, and that $c_0 = 1$. For if $f(x)$ is positive and $c_0 = 1$, that is

$$c_0 = \sigma_{(0)}'' = \sum_{\nu=0}^{k} A_\nu = 1,$$

and only then, the expression (9) represents a frequency-function.

If, in (28), we put $\omega = 1$, we have the usual *B*-type with unit interval

$$f(x) = \sum_{s=0}^{k} \frac{(-1)^s}{s!} \sigma_{(s)}'' \nabla^s \phi(x), \qquad \ldots\ldots(34)$$

where $$\mu_r'' = \bar{\mu}_r - \mu_r'. \qquad \ldots\ldots(35)$$

If, on the other hand, we let $\omega \to 0$, we have

$$\lim_{\omega\to 0} \underset{\omega}{\nabla^s} \phi(x) = \phi^{(s)}(x), \qquad \ldots\ldots(36)$$

so that (28) *contains the A-type as a limiting case.* But the calculation of the coefficients requires special attention, as we have, in the preceding considerations, for instance in (29), assumed $\omega \neq 0$.

Let us, for a moment, put

$$\tau_r = \omega^r \sigma_r'', \qquad \text{......(37)}$$

we obtain then, from (24), putting $s = r - \nu$,

$$\bar{\sigma}_r = \sum_{\nu=0}^{r} \binom{r}{\nu} \tau_\nu \sigma'_{r-\nu}, \qquad \text{......(38)}$$

showing that the τ_ν exist for $\omega \to 0$, provided the $\bar{\sigma}_\nu$ and σ_ν' do.

Now it follows from (18), if we write σ'' instead of σ, and multiply on both sides by ω^r, that

$$\omega^r \sigma_{(r)}'' = \sum_{\nu=0}^{r} \omega^{r-\nu} \tau_\nu \frac{D^\nu 0^{(r)}}{\nu!}.$$

Hence we have, for $\omega \to 0$,

$$\tau_r = \lim_{\omega \to 0} \omega^r \sigma_{(r)}''.$$

We therefore obtain from (28), for $\omega \to 0$,

$$f(x) = \sum_{s=0}^{k} \frac{(-1)^s}{s!} \tau_s \phi^{(s)}(x).$$

We may finally drop the τ-notation; for (38) shows that the τ_ν are calculated from the $\bar{\sigma}_\nu$ and σ_ν' by the same relations as the σ_ν'' for $\omega = 1$. If, therefore, μ_r'' is calculated by

$$\mu_r'' = \bar{\mu}_r - \mu_r', \qquad \text{......(39)}$$

replacing (29) for $\omega \to 0$, we may write $f(x)$ in the form

$$f(x) = \sum_{s=0}^{k} \frac{(-1)^s}{s!} \sigma_s'' \phi^{(s)}(x). \qquad \text{......(40)}$$

Formula (40) is the *A*-type which has thus, together with the *B*-type, been derived from the common source (28).

7. In practice, the question of applying (28) will usually arise under circumstances where an attempt has been made to represent the data by some particular frequency-function $\phi(x)$, but the agreement is not found entirely satisfactory. In that case, if $\phi(x)$ depends on κ constants which have been determined by the method of moments, we have $\bar{\mu}_r = \mu_r'$ for $r = 1, 2, \ldots \kappa$. For the same values of r we therefore have, by (29), $\mu_r'' = 0$, and hence, by (30) and (31), $\sigma_{(r)}'' = 0$, so that the corresponding terms in (28) drop out. It is, at any rate, always advisable to have the same *mean* for $\phi(x)$ and $f(x)$, that is, $\sigma_1' = \bar{\sigma}_1$, or $\sigma_1'' = 0$. From this follows $\sigma_{(r)}'' = m_{(r)}''$ for $r > 1$, so that (28) may be written

$$f(x) = \phi(x) + \sum_{s=2}^{k} \frac{(-1)^s}{s!} \omega^s m_{(s)}'' \underset{\omega}{\nabla^s} \phi(x). \quad \text{......(41)}$$

Under the same circumstances the B-type becomes

$$f(x) = \phi(x) + \sum_{s=2}^{k} \frac{(-1)^s}{s!} m_{(s)}'' \nabla^s \phi(x), \quad \text{......(42)}$$

and the A-type

$$f(x) = \phi(x) + \sum_{s=2}^{k} \frac{(-1)^s}{s!} m_s'' \phi^{(s)}(x). \quad \text{......(43)}$$

It is of course important to remember that these three formulas are only valid if $f(x)$ and $\phi(x)$ have the same mean, that is $\bar{m}_1 = m_1'$.

For use in connection with these formulas we give below the formulas for calculating the six first semi-invariants and factorial moments about the mean, if the moments about the mean are known:

$$\left.\begin{array}{l} \mu_1 = m_1;\ \mu_2 = m_2;\ \mu_3 = m_3 \\ \mu_4 = m_4 - 3m_2^2 \\ \mu_5 = m_5 - 10m_2 m_3 \\ \mu_6 = m_6 - 15m_4 m_2 - 10m_3^2 + 30m_2^3 \end{array}\right\}, \quad \text{......(44)}$$

$$\left.\begin{array}{l} m_{(1)} = m_1;\ m_{(2)} = m_2 \\ m_{(3)} = m_3 - 3m_2 \\ m_{(4)} = m_4 - 6m_3 + 11m_2 \\ m_{(5)} = m_5 - 10m_4 + 35m_3 - 50m_2 \\ m_{(6)} = m_6 - 15m_5 + 85m_4 - 225m_3 + 274m_2 \end{array}\right\} \text{.....(45)}$$

If the frequency-function is continuous, and we use for $\phi(x)$ the normal error-function, the calculation of the coefficients is simplified, as $0 = \mu_3' = \mu_4' = \dots$. We shall not go into this well-known question.

8. Our frequency-function (28) is, on the conditions indicated above, a genuine frequency-function, not a mere approximation to one. Yet it has the *form* of a number of terms of a series and has the advantage that if the fit is not found satisfactory, another term may be added to those present, without it being necessary to start the calculations all over again. Further, the calculation of the constants is as simple as may be desired.

There are, however, considerable drawbacks. We cannot, as with Pearson's types, be sure beforehand that negative values will not occur; as a matter of fact they often do occur, and this can only be ascertained at the end of the calculation. We have not even very good reason to expect that by adding another term such negative values may be made to disappear. It was, furthermore, pointed out by Edgeworth that the terms in the *A*-series are not arranged according to their order of magnitude. The re-arranged *A*-series involves an entirely different problem which has been studied recently by H. Cramér in a very thorough paper to which I would like to call attention*.

It may finally be observed that the frequency-function (28) often presents several maxima and minima. This may be an advantage if the experience also does so; but then, such an experience is often of little value, as the presence of maxima and minima is, perhaps, due to the fact that the material is not homogeneous, or too small. We are therefore inclined to think that the apparent generality of (28) is rather a disadvantage than otherwise, and that Pearson's types are as a rule preferable.

* H. Cramér, "On the composition of elementary errors," *Skandinavisk Aktuarietidskrift* (1928), pp. 13–74 and pp. 141–180. Some applications of the theory are given in a paper by the same author, "On the Mathematical Theory of Risk," pp. 48–65, published in *Försäkringsaktiebolaget Skandia, 1855–1930*, II, Stockholm, 1930.

NOTATION

As the author's notation for moments and similar frequency constants differs from the usual English notation*, it has been found advisable to give the following summary of the author's notation:

rth moment about origin: σ_r.
rth ,, ,, mean: m_r, for $r > 1$.

For $r = 1$ the author defines $m_1 = \sigma_1$.

rth factorial moment about origin: $\sigma_{(r)}$.
rth ,, ,, ,, mean: $m_{(r)}$, for $r > 1$.

For $r = 1$ the author defines $m_{(1)} = \sigma_{(1)}$.

rth semi-invariant: μ_r.

All five symbols refer to a total frequency of unity.

If the moments are not "observed values" but so-called "true values," a bar is placed above the leading letter, thus:

$$\bar{\sigma}_r, \bar{m}_r, \bar{\sigma}_{(r)}, \bar{m}_{(r)}, \bar{\mu}_r.$$

Moments referring to the function $\phi(x)$ are, however, distinguished by a dash:

$$\sigma_r', m_r', \sigma_{(r)}', m_{(r)}', \mu_r',$$

and moments referring to A_ν, considered as a function of ν, by a double-dash:

$$\sigma_r'', m_r'', \sigma_{(r)}'', m_{(r)}'', \mu_r''.$$

* In the usual English notation
ν_r is used for the author's m_r,
μ_r ,, ,, ,, ,, $\bar{m}_r$,
$\nu_1 = \mu_1 = 0$,
and σ is used for the standard deviation.

INDEX

Annuities, annuities-certain, 32; life, 9–11, 26–29, 32; increasing life, 32; temporary life, 32, 33
Approximations, 1, 12, 13, 20, 22, 23, 28, 29

Bertelsen, N. P., 19
Biometric functions, 2–9; e_x, 4–8, 31; l_x, 3–11, 23, 26; μ_x, 2–11, 23, 29, 33; p_x, 3–11; q_x, 3–11
Bortkiewicz, L. v., 32
Bruns, H., 37

Charlier, C. V. L., 37–39
Compatibility of frequency-constants, 19
Continuous functions, 35, 38–40, 42, 47
Contradictions, 1, 4, 15, 16, 19, 20
Convergence, 26, 39
Cramér, H., 48

Derivates of l_x, 23, 26; D_x, 26; normal error-function, 38; $\phi(x)$, 45–47
Determination of constants in frequency-functions, 15–17, 20, 39, 44–47
Development in a series, 37–39
Difference table of $\sin \frac{x}{10}$, 21
Differences of Poisson's frequency-function, 38; $\phi(x)$, 44–47
Discontinuous functions, 35, 40, 42, 43
Divergence, of moments of Charlier's function, 39

Edgeworth, F. Y., 37, 48
Elderton, W. P., 35, 41
Endowment assurances, policy values of, 33
Equivalence, of various classes of frequency-constants, 12, 14, 42; moments to observations, 12
Errors, 7, 28; Gauss' Law of, 15, 47; normal error-function, 47; theory of, 7; mean, 15
Euler, 26
Expectation of life, 4–8, 31; death, 3; mathematical, 3, 12, 13, 18

Factorial moments, 41, 42, 47
Fisher, R. A., 18
Force of mortality, 2–11, 23, 31–33
Free policy, in the case of a pure endowment, 34
Frequency-constants, 11–20
Frequency-functions, 2, 15, 20, 35–48
Friedli, W., 28
Functions, discontinuous, 35, 40, 42, 43; gamma, 37; generating, 24, 40; monotonic, 3; non-decreasing, 4, 5, 7, 33; non-increasing, 5, 29, 33; positive, 29; undefined, 22

Gamma functions, 37
Gauss, 12, 13, 15–17, 20, 38, 40
Generating functions, 24, 40
Graduation, 1, 8, 22, 39
Gumbel, E. J., 32

Imaginary values of observations, 19; constants characterizing observations, 37; frequency-functions, 18
Increasing life-annuities, 32
Inequalities, 1, 4–10, 25–34; a general proposition, 29, 30; between moments, 31; between integrals, 30
Infinite durations, 7
Integrals, repeated, 3; inequalities between, 30
Intercalation, 22, 23
Interpolation, 1, 8, 22, 23

Least squares, method of, 15
Life-annuities, 9–11, 26–28, 32, 33
Life-assurances, equal policy values of, 9
Limits, 2, 4, 6, 10, 12, 22, 23, 26, 28, 32

Makeham's formula, 6, 8, 9, 11, 23, 26
Mathematical expectation, 3, 12, 18
Maxima and minima of frequency-functions, 48
Mean, 11, 47; error, 15; theorem of mean value, 27; weighted, 29
Moments, 3, 11–19, 31, 41, 46
Monotonic functions, 3
Mortality Tables, $O^{M(5)}$ table, 6, 8, 28, 29; H^M table, 11; producing the same policy values, 9

Non-decreasing functions, 4, 5, 7, 33
Non-increasing functions, 5, 29, 33
Notation for frequency-constants, 49

"Oldest age," doctrine of, 6

Paid-up policies, in the case of a pure endowment, 34
Pearson, Karl, 32, 35, 36, 37, 40, 48
Poisson, 38
Policy values of endowment assurances, 33; different mortality tables producing the same, 9
Polynomials $G_n(\zeta, \theta)$, 24–27
Positive functions, 29
Presumptive values of frequency-constants, 11–20
Probabilities, 6, 7, 11, 20, 39, 40; of dying, 3; of surviving, 3
Pure endowments, paid-up policies in the case of, 34

Remainder term, 23, 26–29, 32

Semi-invariants, 11, 14, 19, 41, 43, 47
Series: *A*-series, 38–48; *B*-series, 38–48
Sheppard, W. F., 41
Significant figures, 8
Smoothness, 8
Standard deviation, 14, 18, 19
Steffensen, J. F., 2, 16, 22, 23, 29, 31, 39, 40, 41, 44
Symmetrical functions of observations, 11

Table of sin $\frac{x}{10}$, 21
Taylor's theorem, 24
Tchebychef, 30
Thiele, T. N., 12, 14, 20, 37
True values, of frequency-constants, 12
Tschuprow, A. A., 18, 20

Undefined functions, 22

Weighted mean, 29

For EU product safety concerns, contact us at Calle de José Abascal, 56–1°, 28003 Madrid, Spain or eugpsr@cambridge.org.

www.ingramcontent.com/pod-product-compliance
Ingram Content Group UK Ltd.
Pitfield, Milton Keynes, MK11 3LW, UK
UKHW041124151225
465965UK00016B/13
* 9 7 8 1 3 1 6 6 0 1 9 1 4 *